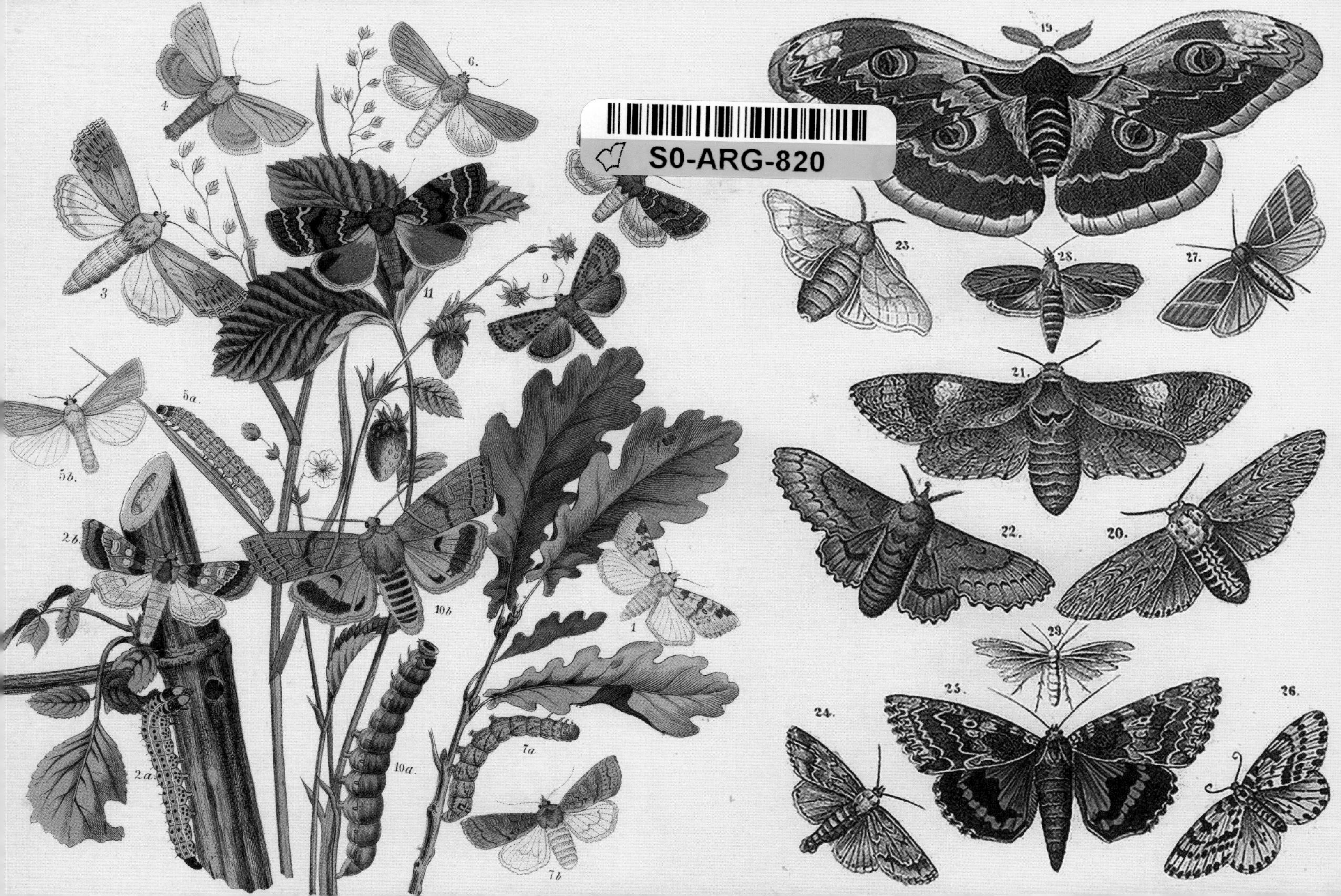
4
6.
3
11
9
5a.
5b.
2b.
10b
1
2a.
10a.
7a
7b
19.
23.
28.
27.
21.
22.
20.
29.
25.
26.
24.

Also look for the other books in the Giggle and Learn series by the same author:
WE DIG WORMS, THE REAL POOP ON PIGEONS!, SNAILS ARE JUST MY SPEED!, SOMETHING'S FISHY, ANTS DON'T WEAR PANTS!

For Zoe McCloskey, my creative daughter, and her amazing friends.

Editorial Director & Senior Designer: FRANÇOISE MOULY

Executive Editor: TUCKER STONE

KEVIN McCLOSKEY'S artwork was painted with acrylics and gouache on Canson colored papers.

A TOON BOOK

A TOON Book™ © 2023 Kevin McCloskey & TOON Books, an imprint of Astra Books for Young Readers, a division of Astra Publishing House. With thanks to Rebecca Lawrence and Dr. Gregory Setliff for their expert opinions. Historical prints are chromolithographs by Emil Hochanz, published in 1877, and from *Naturgeschichte für schule und haus*, 1871. Copying or digitizing this book for storage, display, or distribution in any other medium is strictly prohibited. All rights reserved. For information about permission to reproduce selections from this book, please contact permissions@astrapublishinghouse.com. TOON Books®, TOON Graphics™, and TOON Into Reading!™ are trademarks of Astra Publishing House.

Library of Congress Cataloging-in-Publication Data: Names: McCloskey, Kevin, author, illustrator. Title: Caterpillars : what will I be when I get to be me? / Kevin McCloskey. Description: New York, NY : TOON Books, [2023] | Series: Giggle and learn | Audience: Grades K-1 | Summary: "A group of diverse children explore how caterpillars morph into moths and butterflies"– Provided by publisher. Identifiers: LCCN 2022048584 | ISBN 9781662665080 (hardcover) | ISBN 9781662665097 (trade paperback) | ISBN 9781662665103 (ebook) Subjects: LCSH: Caterpillars–Morphology–Juvenile literature. Classification: LCC QL544.2 .M317 2023 | DDC 595.78/9--dc23/eng/20221018 LC record available at https://lccn.loc.gov/2022048584   All our books are Smyth Sewn (the highest library-quality binding available) and printed with soy-based inks on acid-free, woodfree paper harvested from responsible sources. Printed in China. First edition.   ISBN 978-1-6626-6508-0 (hardcover)   ISBN 978-1-6626-6509-7 (paperback)

10 9 8 7 6 5 4 3 2 1

Caterpillars:

What will I be when I get to be me?

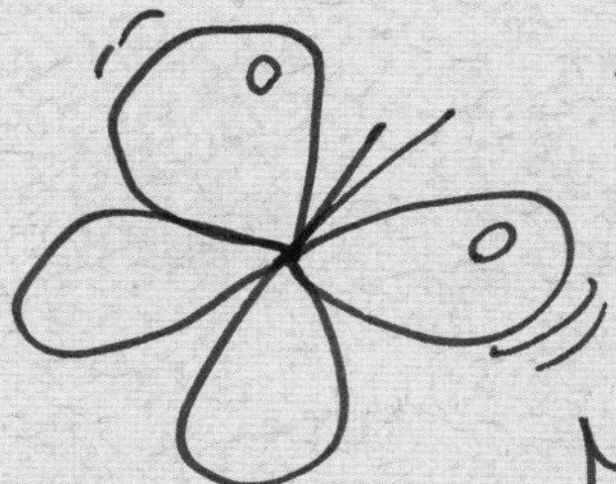

for Grace —
Kevin McCloskey
2023

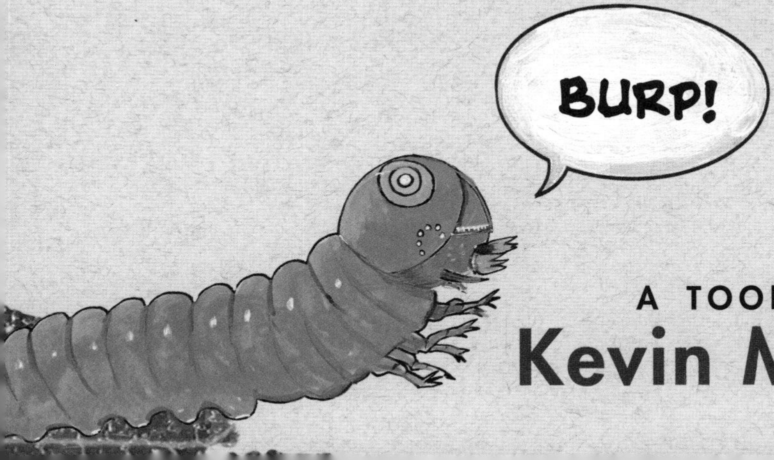
BURP!

A TOON BOOK BY

Kevin McCloskey

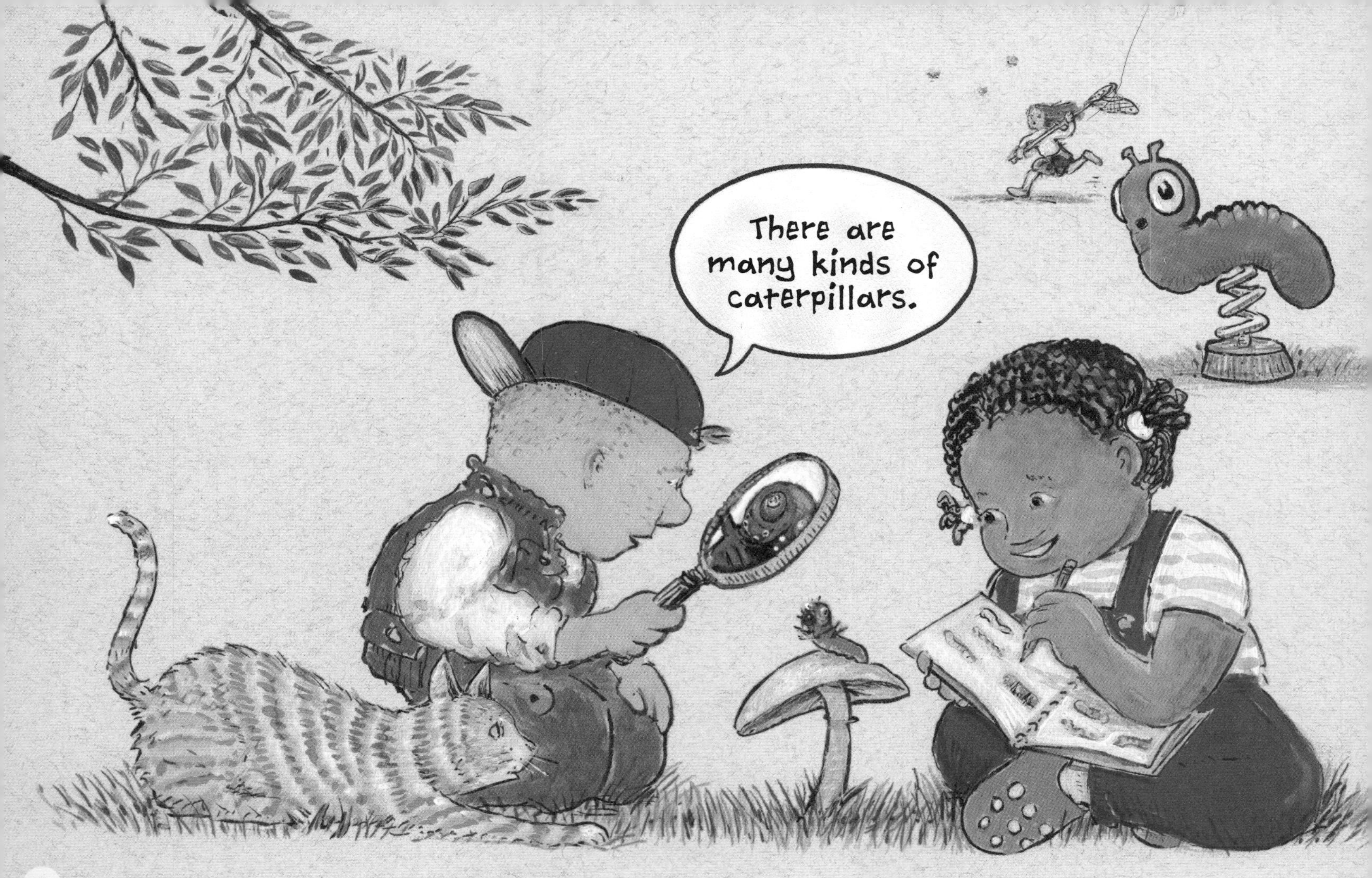
There are many kinds of caterpillars.

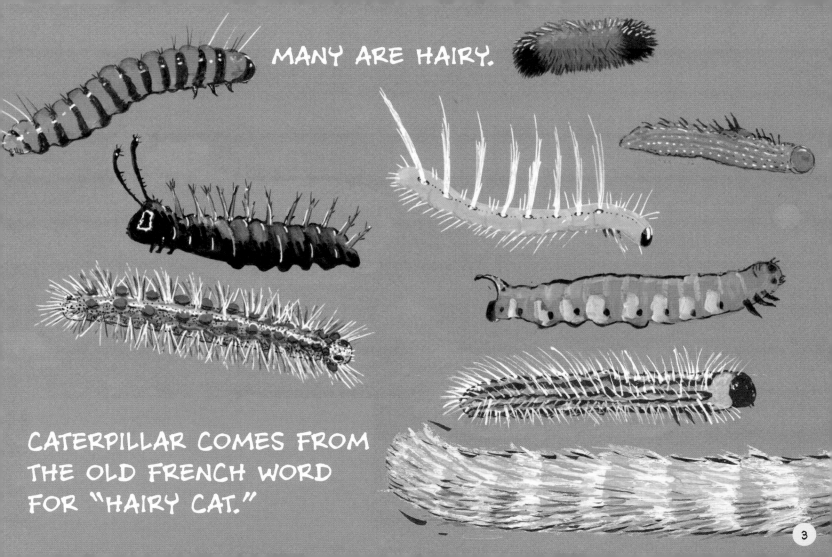

MANY ARE HAIRY.

CATERPILLAR COMES FROM
THE OLD FRENCH WORD
FOR "HAIRY CAT."

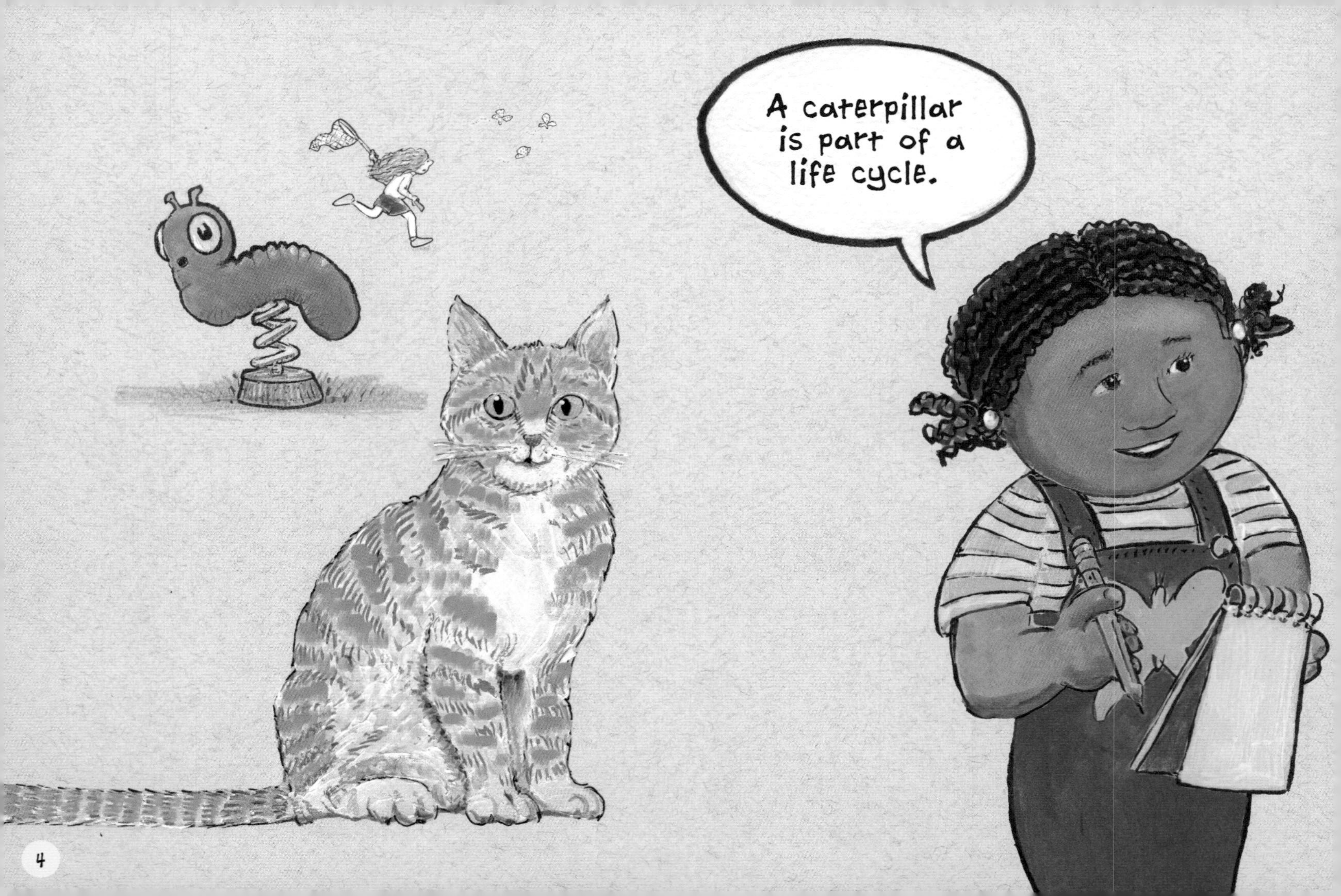
A caterpillar is part of a life cycle.

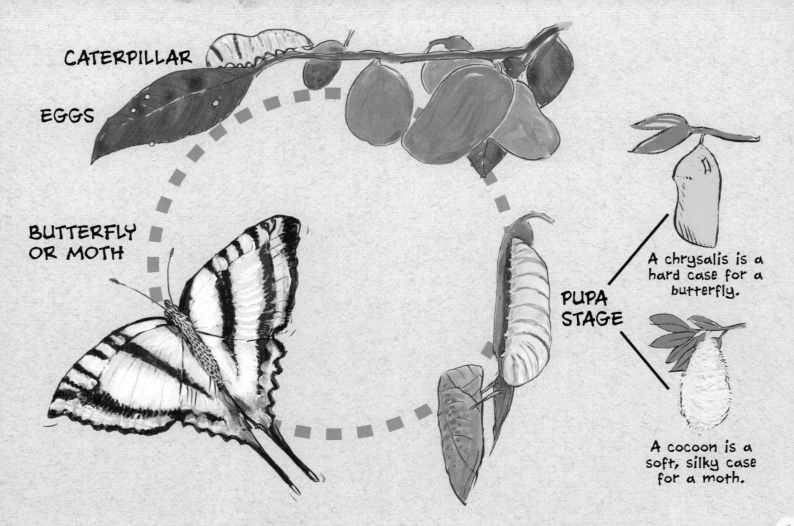

CATERPILLAR

EGGS

BUTTERFLY
OR MOTH

PUPA
STAGE

A chrysalis is a
hard case for a
butterfly.

A cocoon is a
soft, silky case
for a moth.

THE STORY STARTS WITH EGGS ON LEAVES.

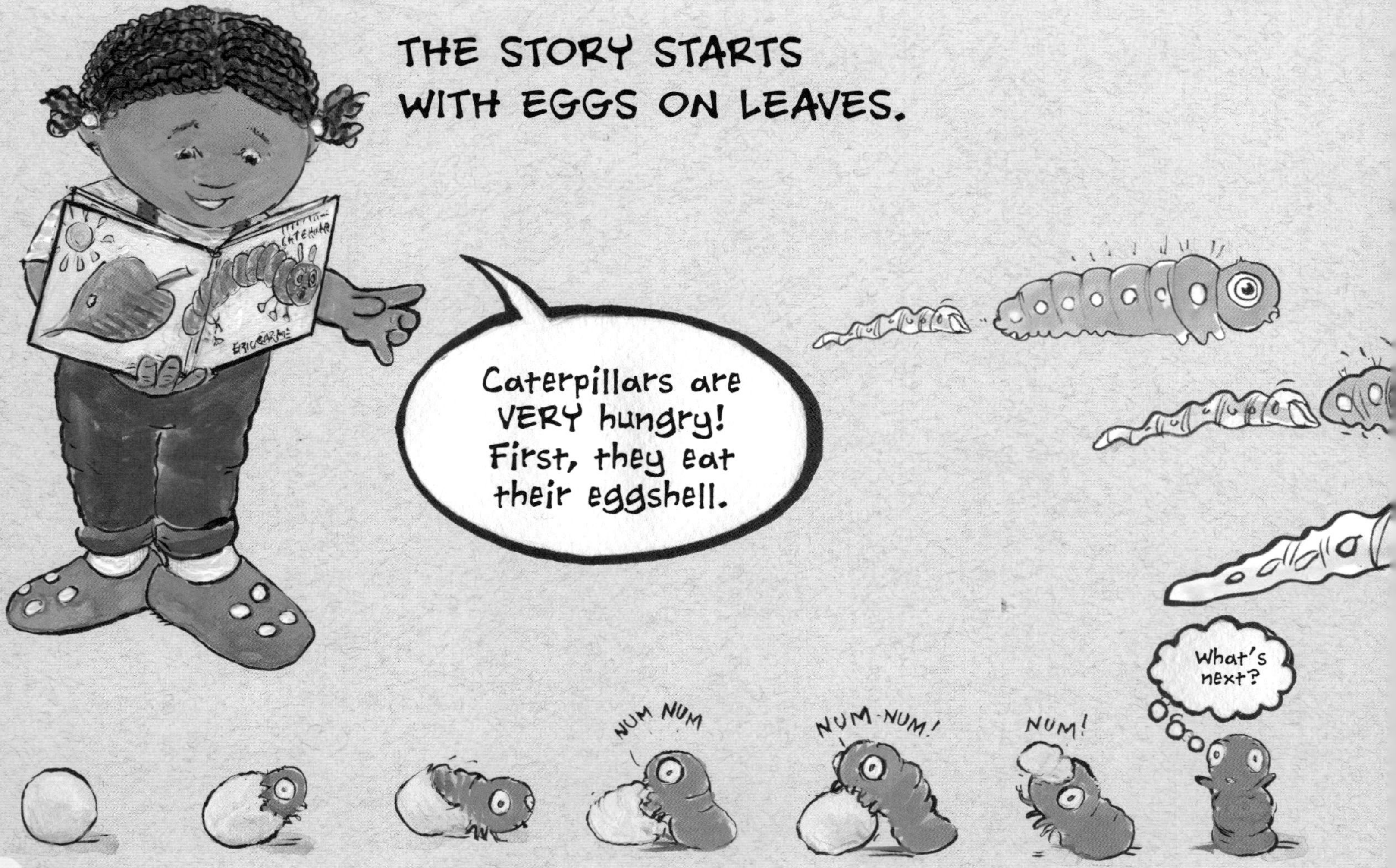
Caterpillars are VERY hungry! First, they eat their eggshell.
NUM NUM
NUM-NUM!
NUM!
What's next?

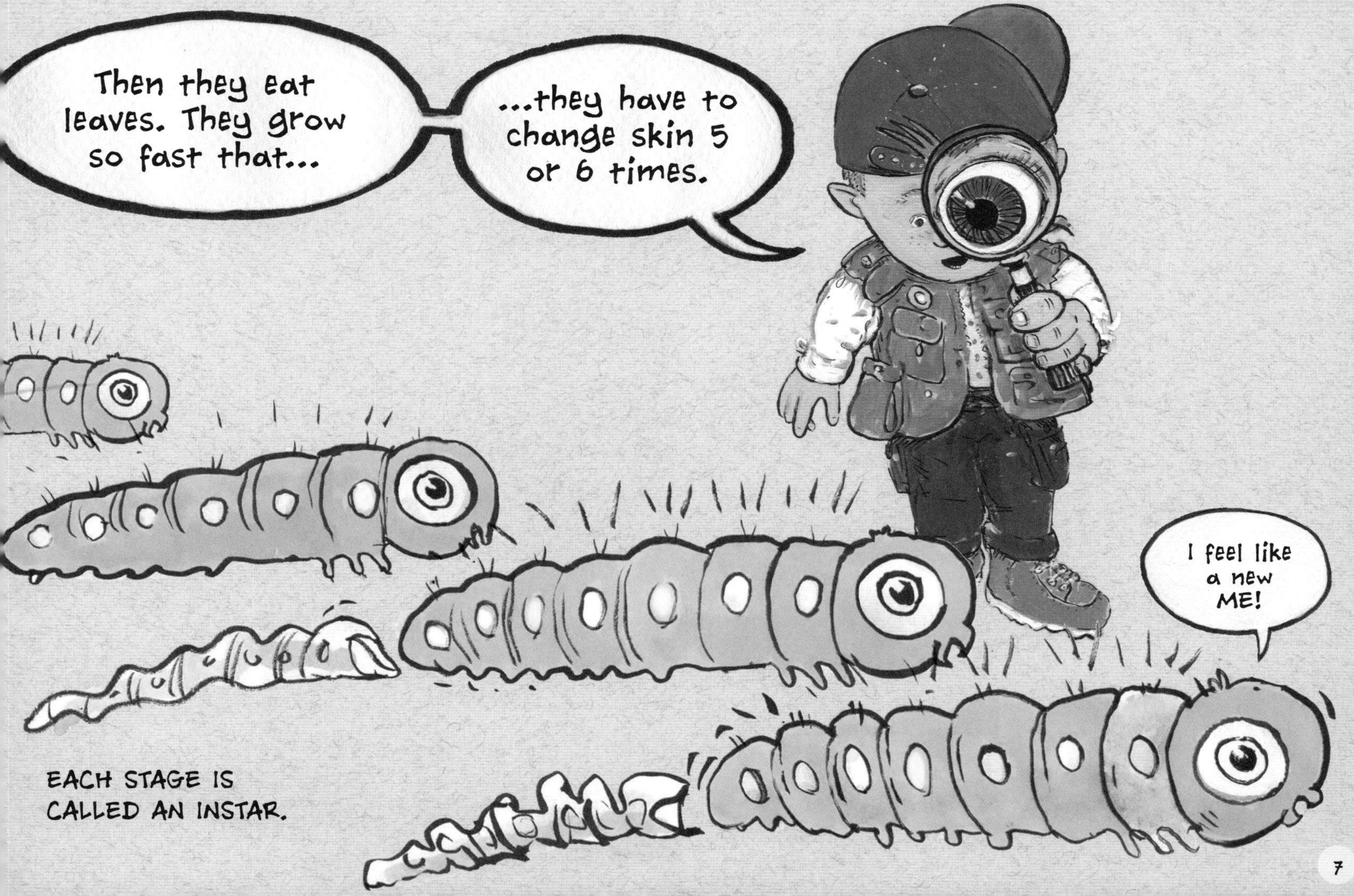
Then they eat leaves. They grow so fast that...
...they have to change skin 5 or 6 times.
I feel like a new ME!

EACH STAGE IS CALLED AN INSTAR.

A CATERPILLAR IS A TUBE WITH A STOMACH.

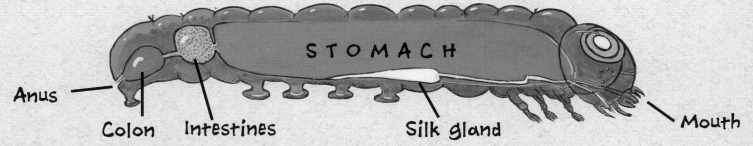

STOMACH

Anus

Colon   Intestines

Silk gland

Mouth

False eye

Eye spots

Mandibles are good to chomp on the edges of leaves.

Spinneret to spin silk

CATERPILLARS CAN MOVE FROM TREES BY HANGING ON LINES OF SILK. AND WHEN MANY CATERPILLARS DROP...

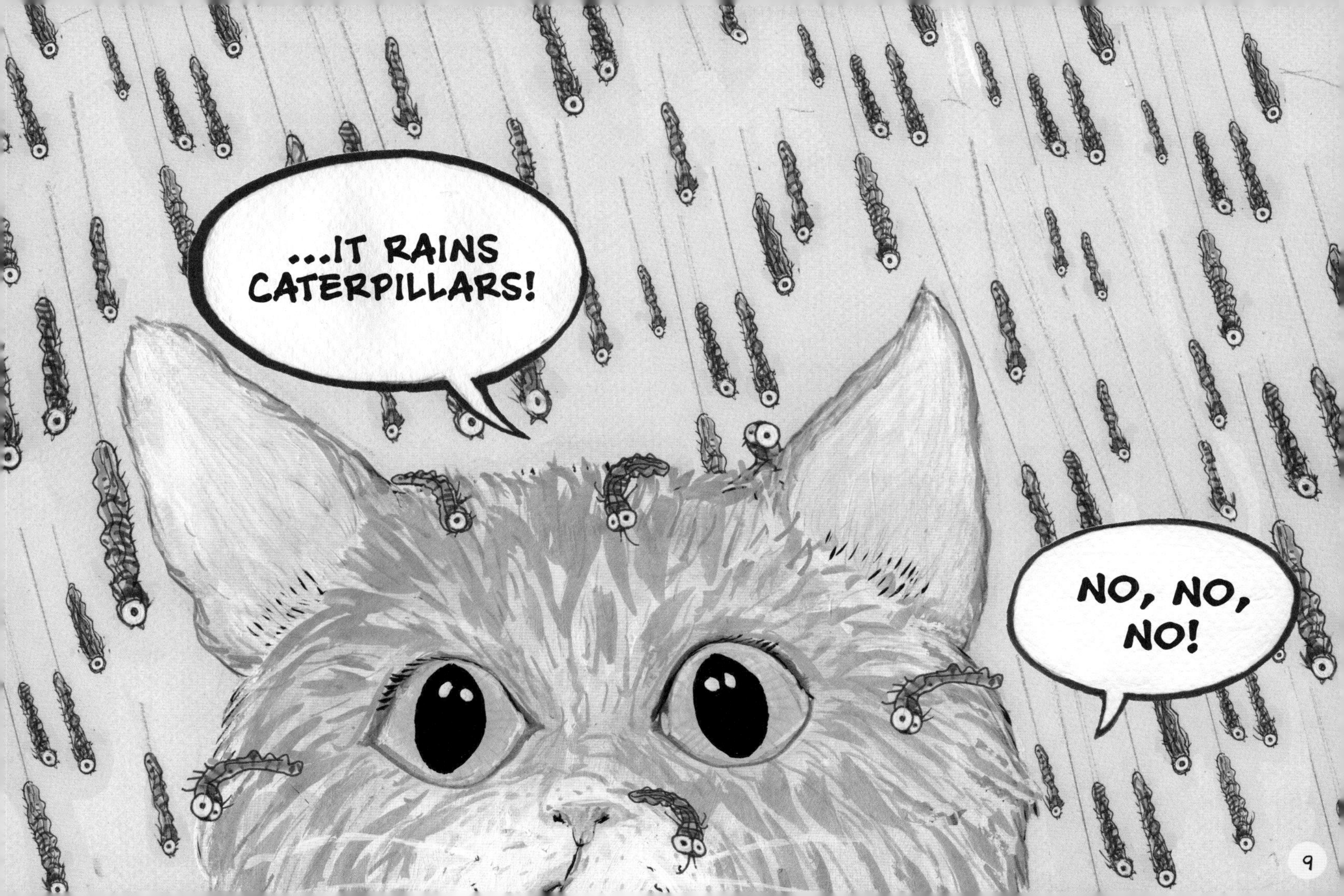
...IT RAINS CATERPILLARS!
NO, NO, NO!

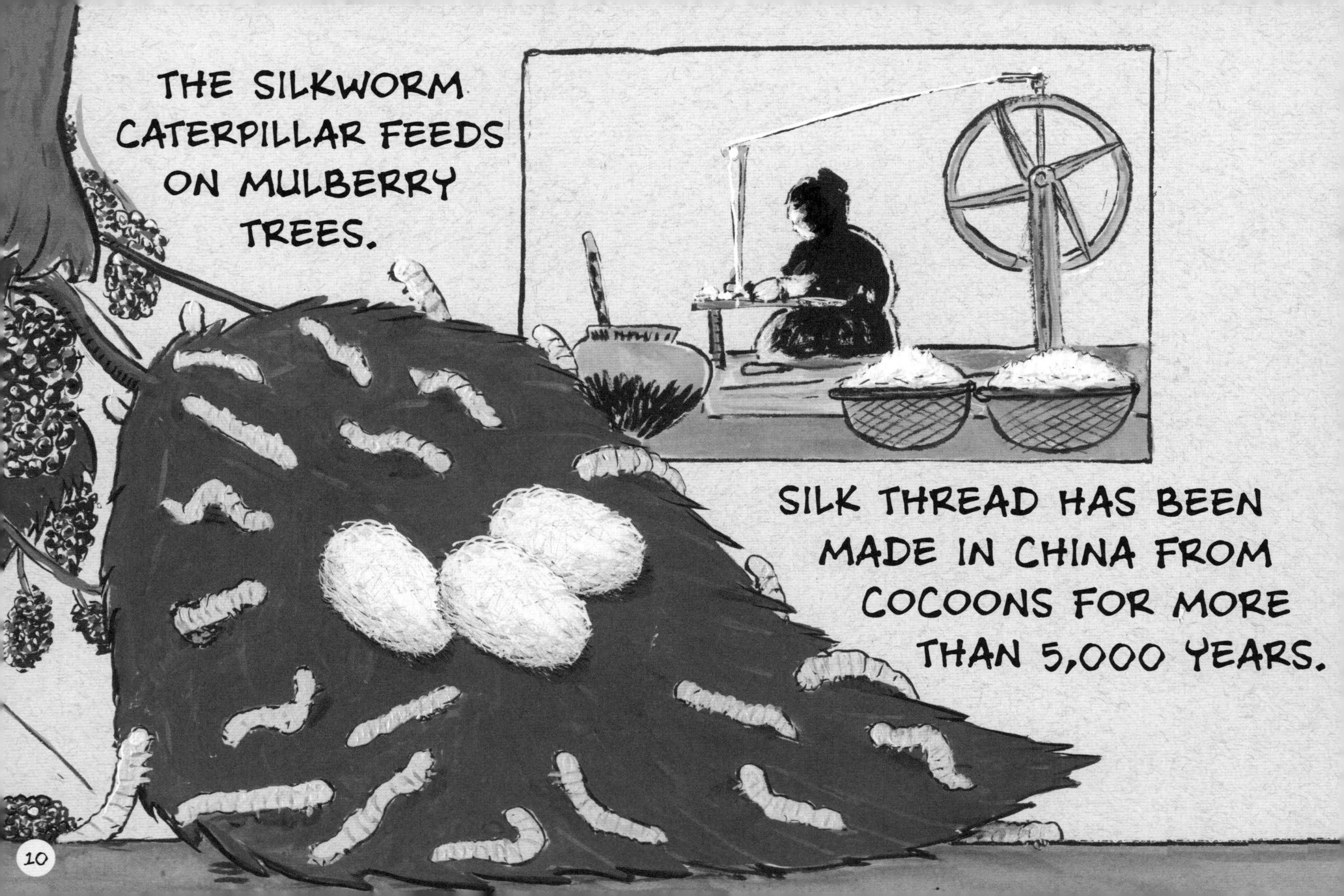

THE SILKWORM CATERPILLAR FEEDS ON MULBERRY TREES.

SILK THREAD HAS BEEN MADE IN CHINA FROM COCOONS FOR MORE THAN 5,000 YEARS.

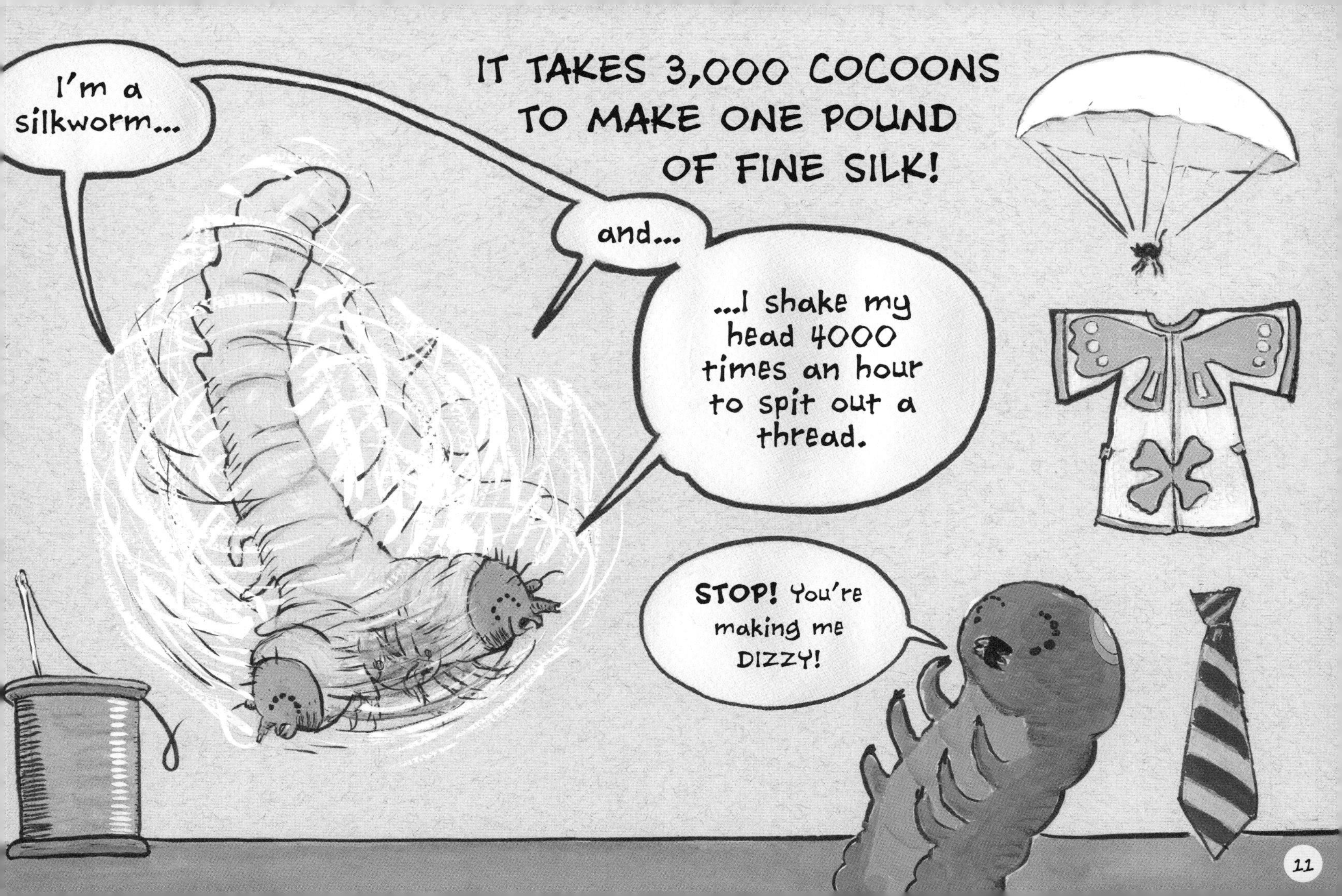
IT TAKES 3,000 COCOONS TO MAKE ONE POUND OF FINE SILK!
I'm a silkworm...
and...
...I shake my head 4000 times an hour to spit out a thread.
STOP! You're making me DIZZY!

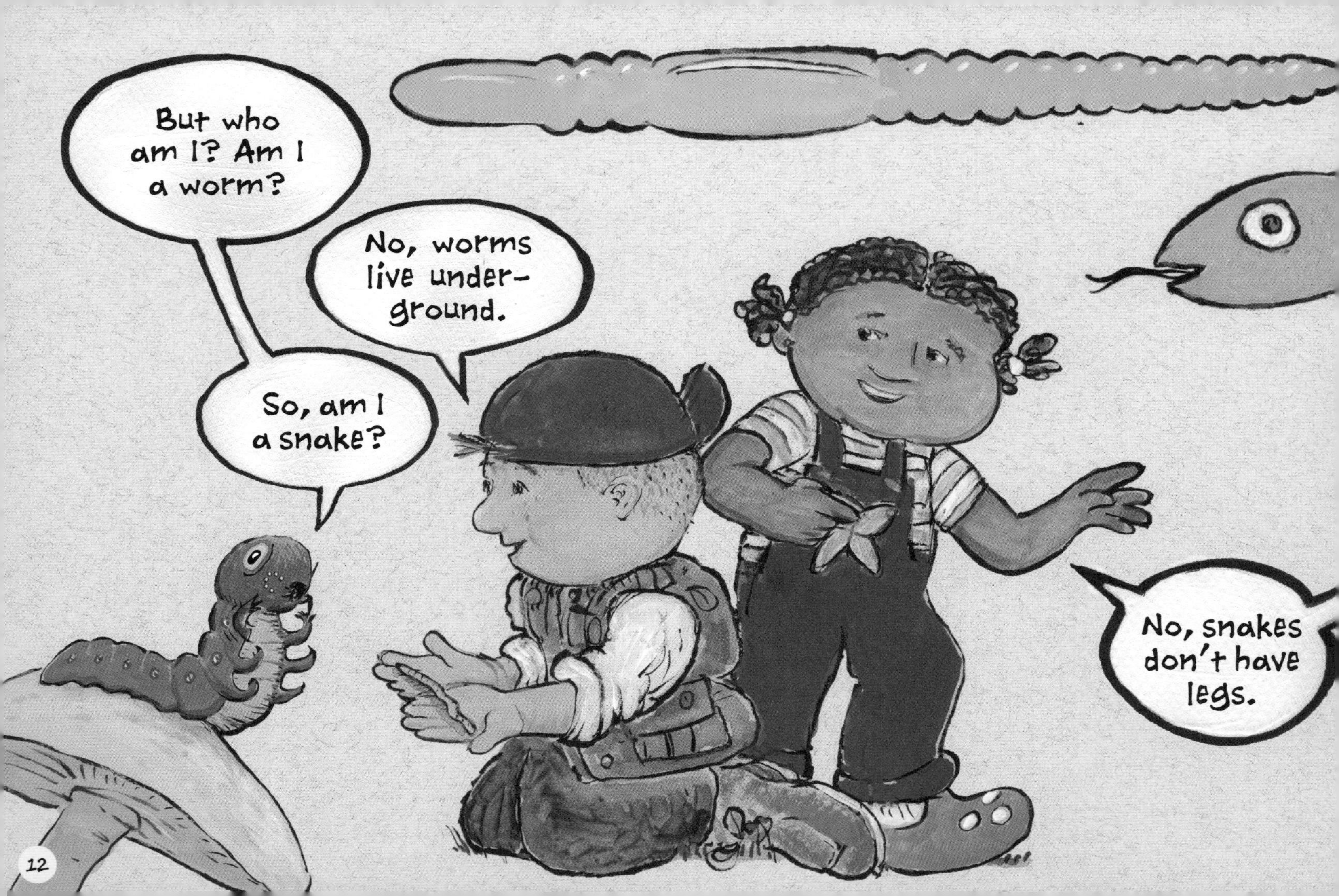
But who am I? Am I a worm?
No, worms live under-ground.
So, am I a snake?
No, snakes don't have legs.

Snakes have bones, unlike worms or caterpillars.

You are an insect. You have six legs.

And you walk in a funny way.

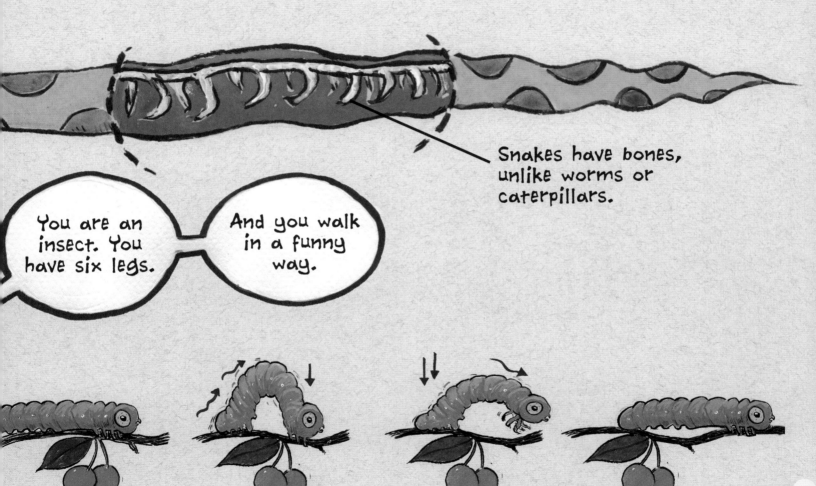

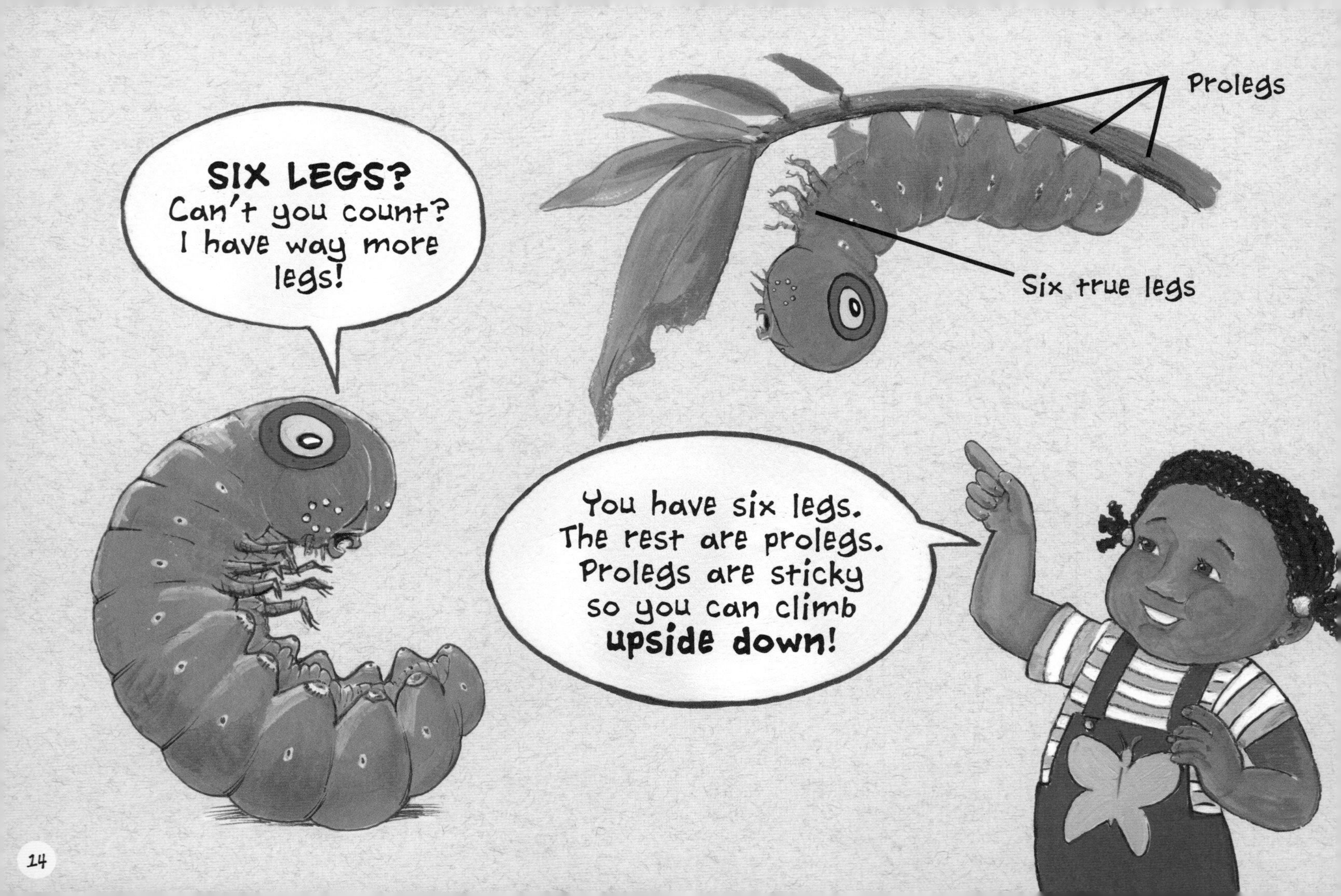
SIX LEGS? Can't you count? I have way more legs!
Prolegs
Six true legs
You have six legs. The rest are prolegs. Prolegs are sticky so you can climb **upside down!**

AND THEN,
ONE DAY,
THE ANSWER
COMES...

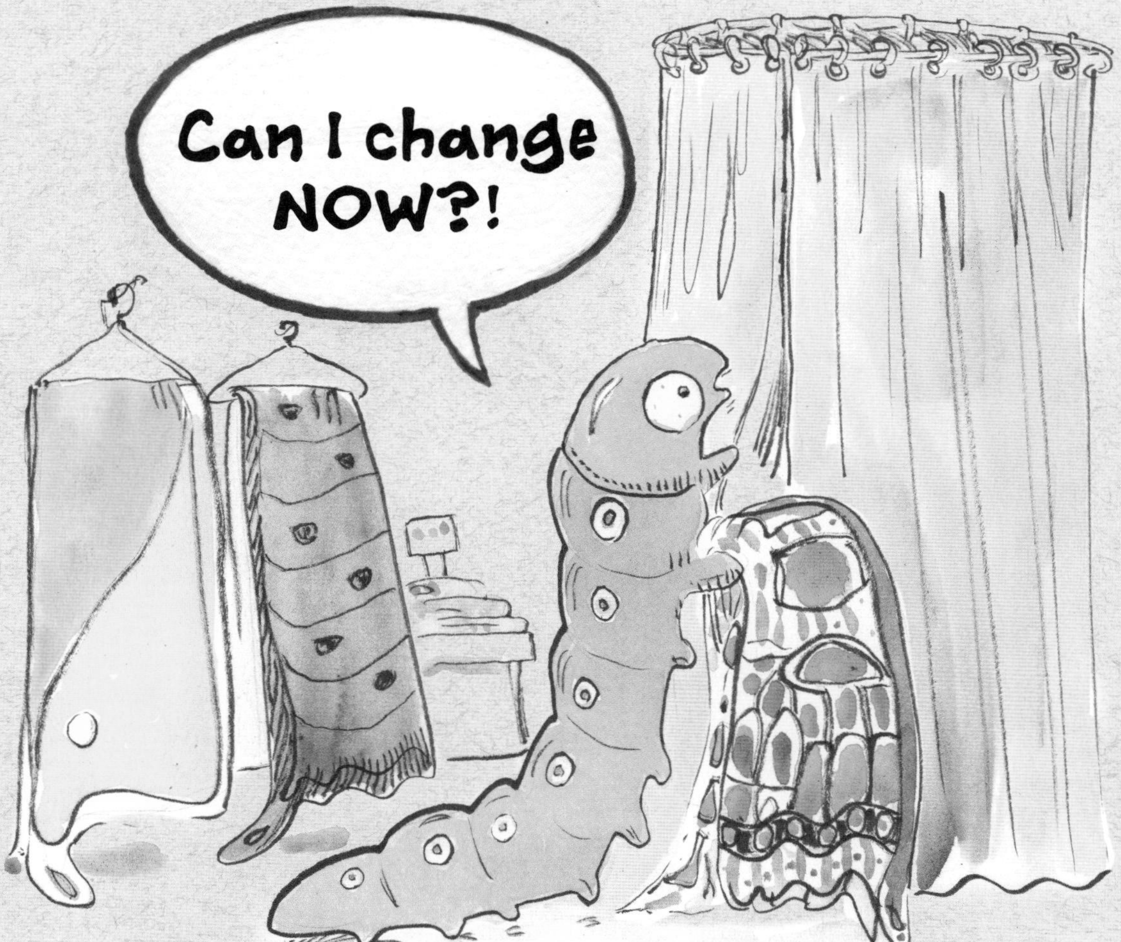
Can I change NOW?!

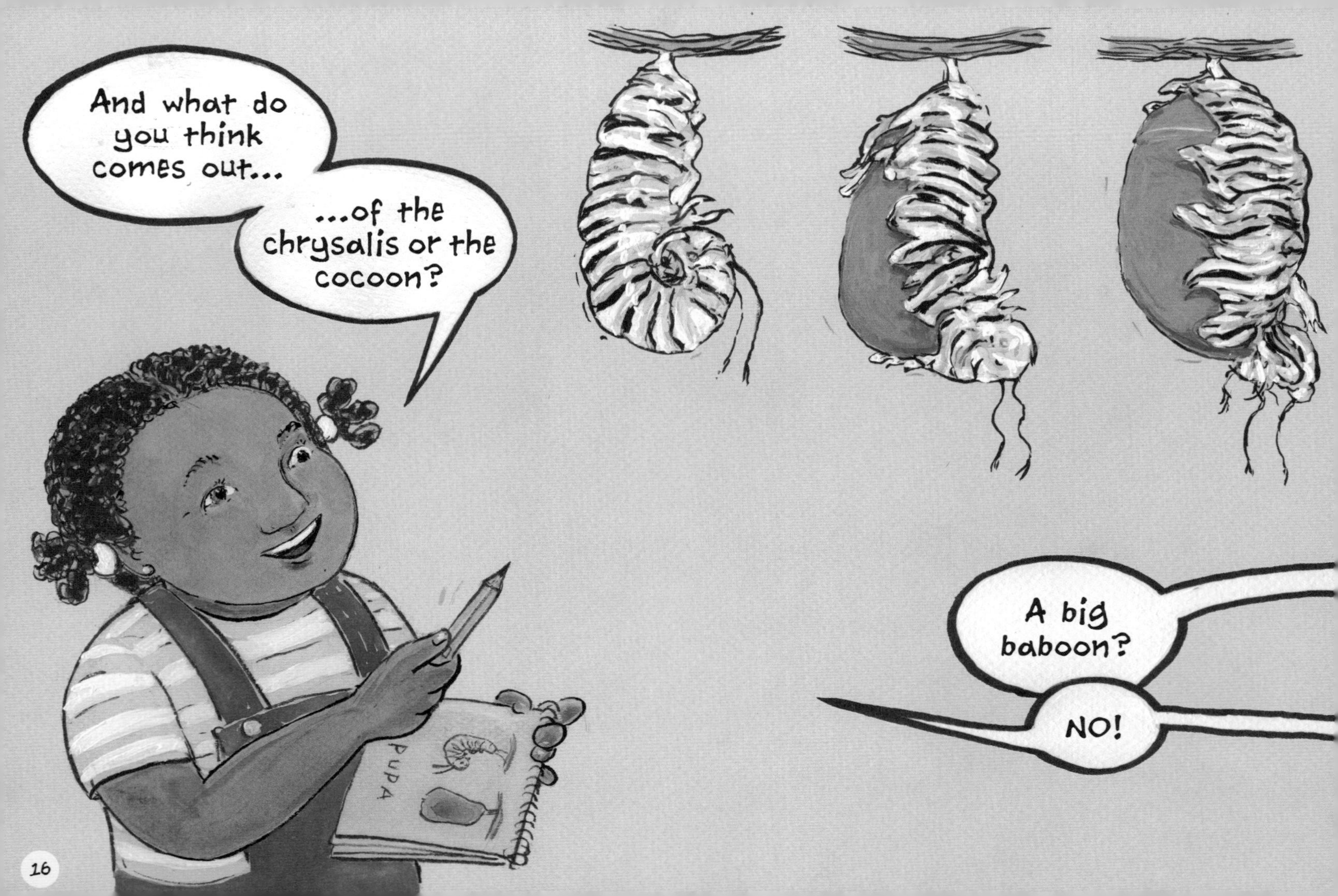
And what do you think comes out...
...of the chrysalis or the cocoon?
PUPA
A big baboon?
NO!

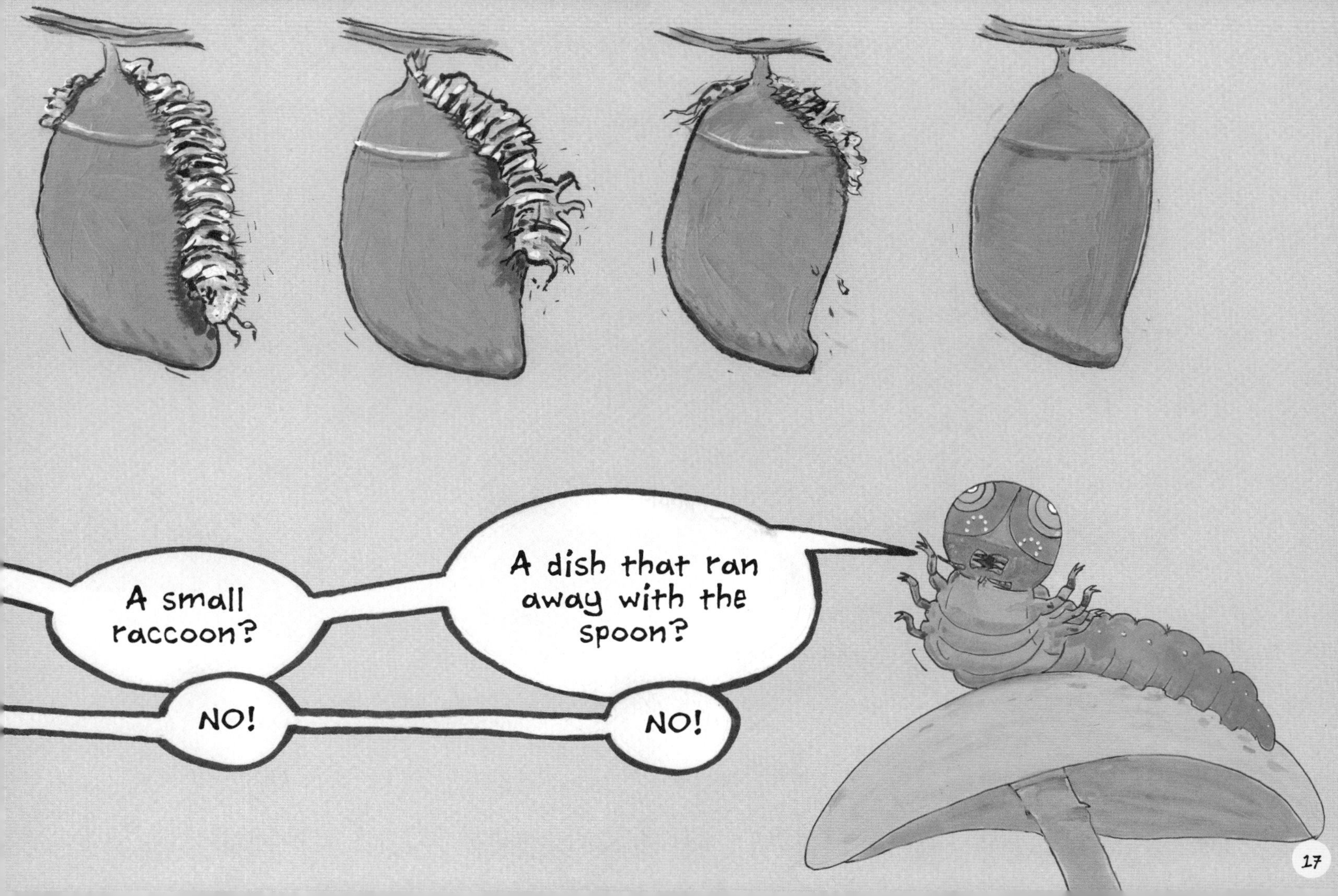
A small raccoon?
A dish that ran away with the spoon?
NO!
NO!

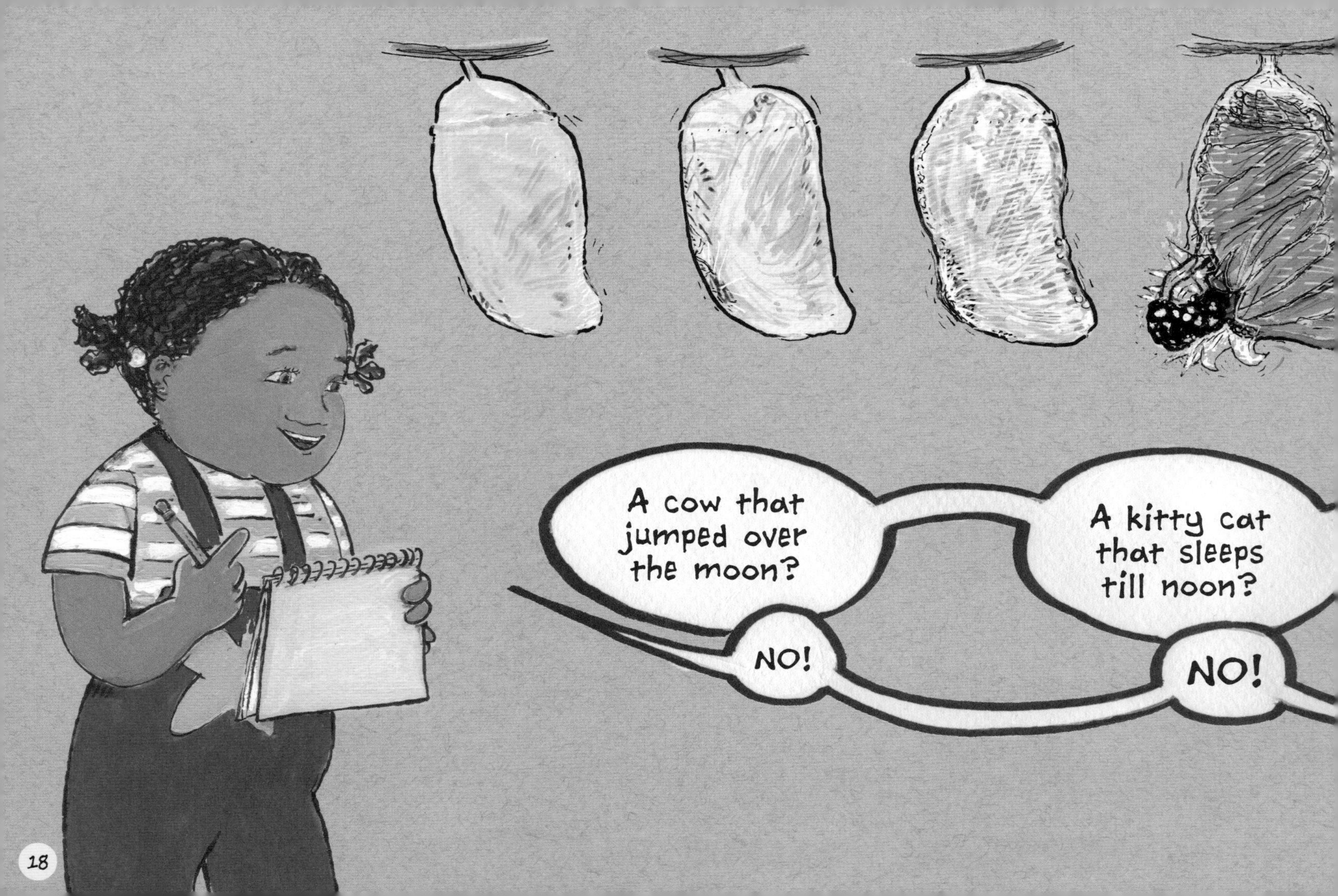
A cow that jumped over the moon?
NO!
A kitty cat that sleeps till noon?
NO!

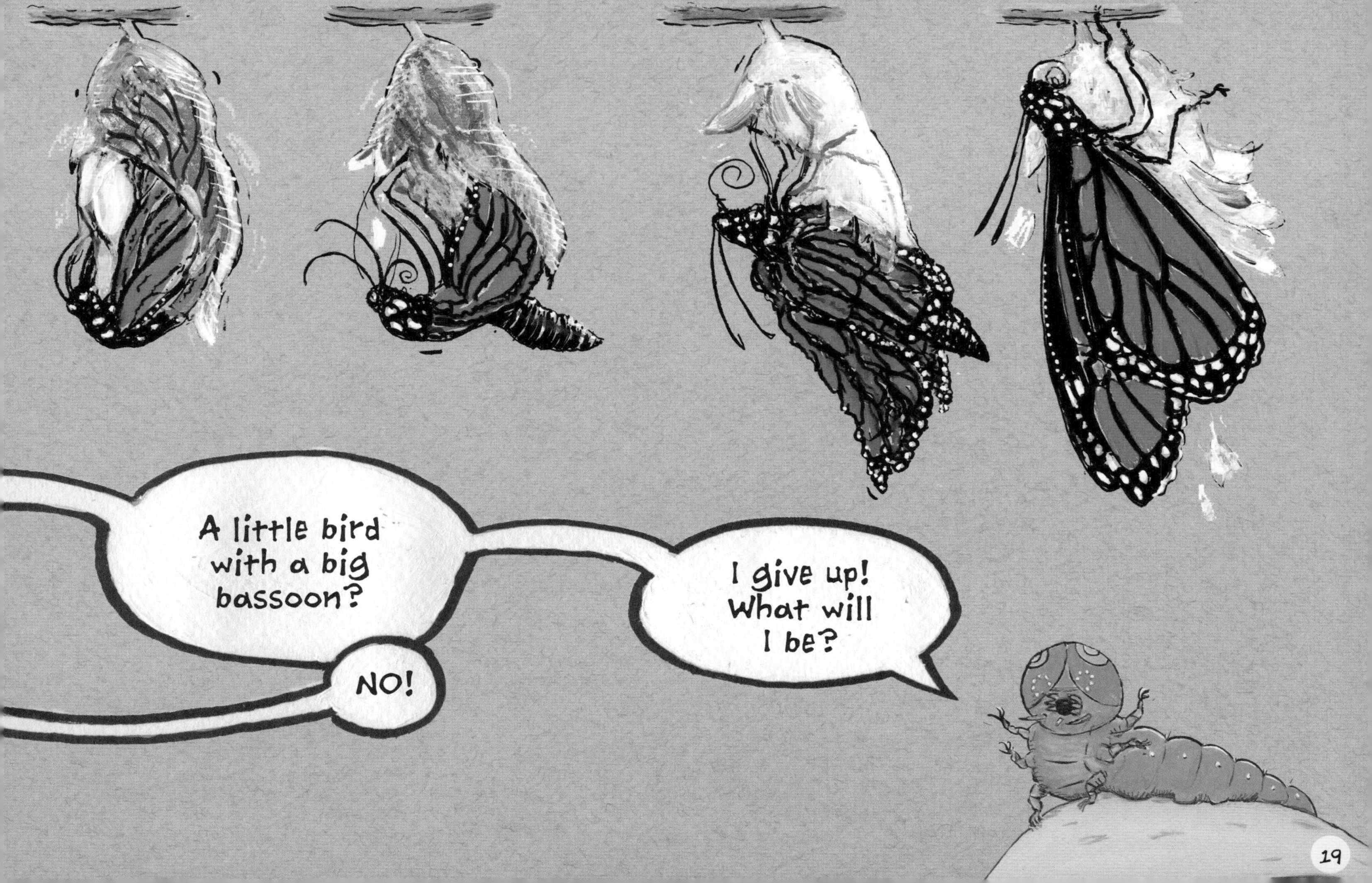
A little bird with a big bassoon?
NO!
I give up! What will I be?

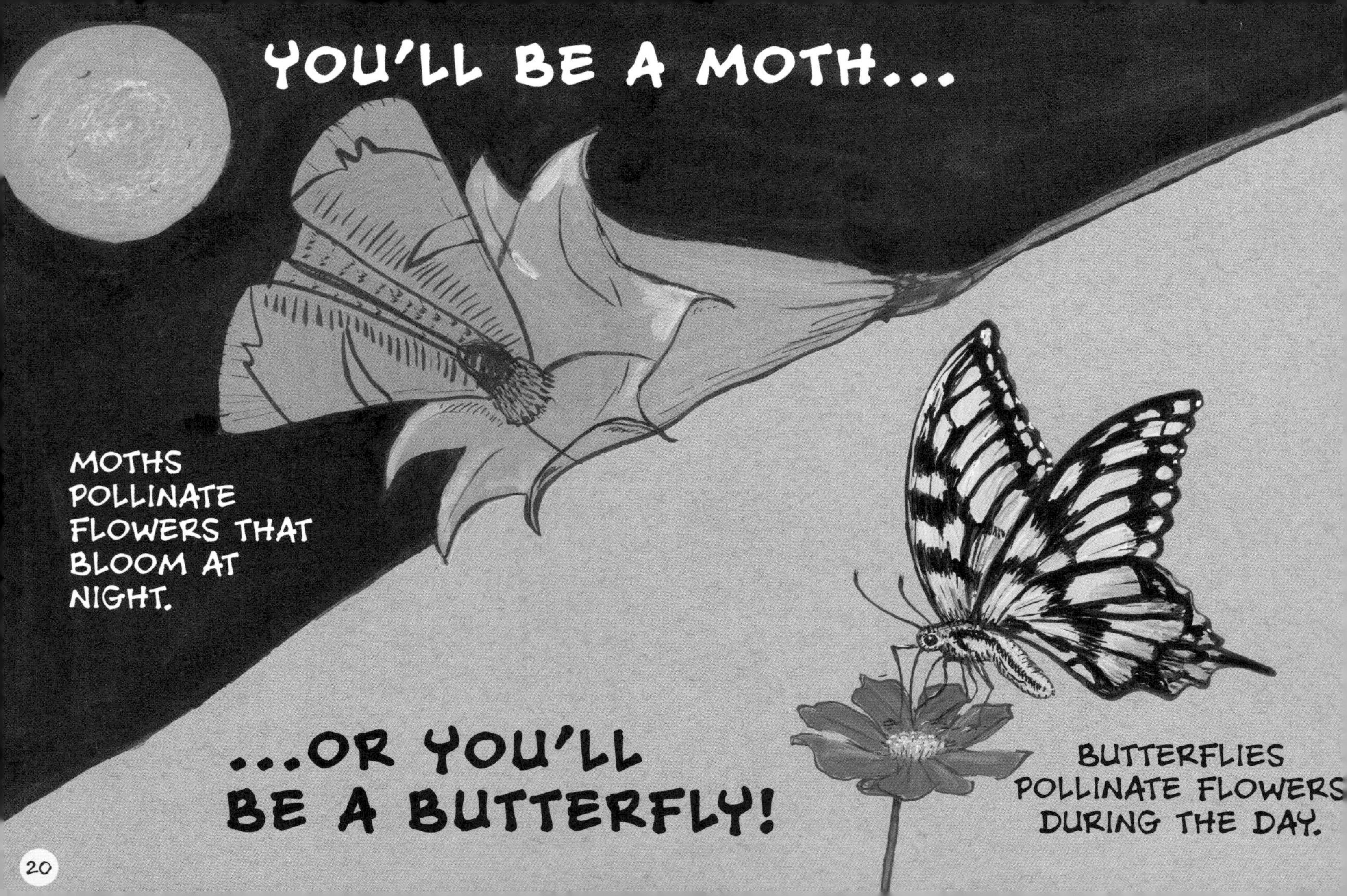
YOU'LL BE A MOTH...
MOTHS POLLINATE FLOWERS THAT BLOOM AT NIGHT.
...OR YOU'LL BE A BUTTERFLY!
BUTTERFLIES POLLINATE FLOWERS DURING THE DAY.

MOTHS AND BUTTERFLIES CAN LOOK A LOT ALIKE.

MOTHS REST WITH THEIR WINGS FLAT.

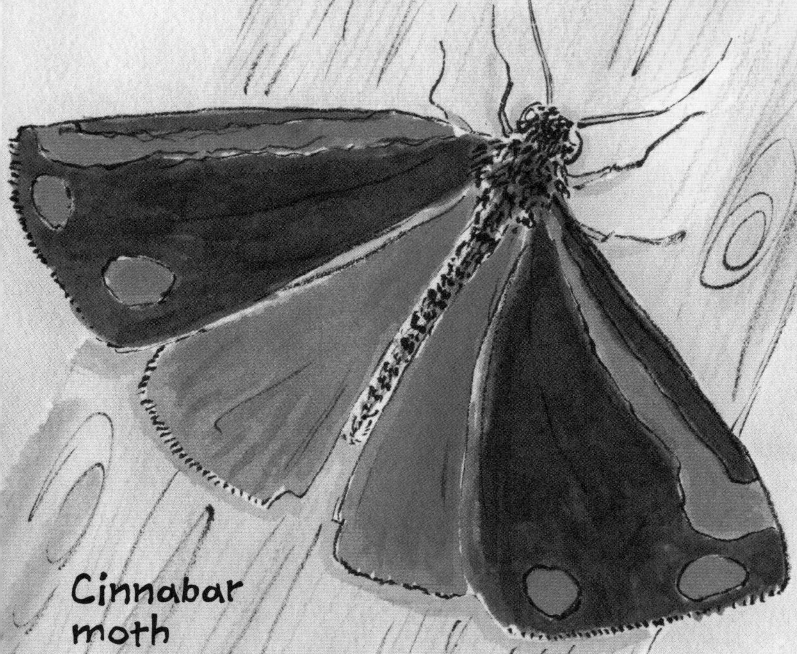

Cinnabar moth

BUTTERFLIES REST WITH THEIR WINGS FOLDED.

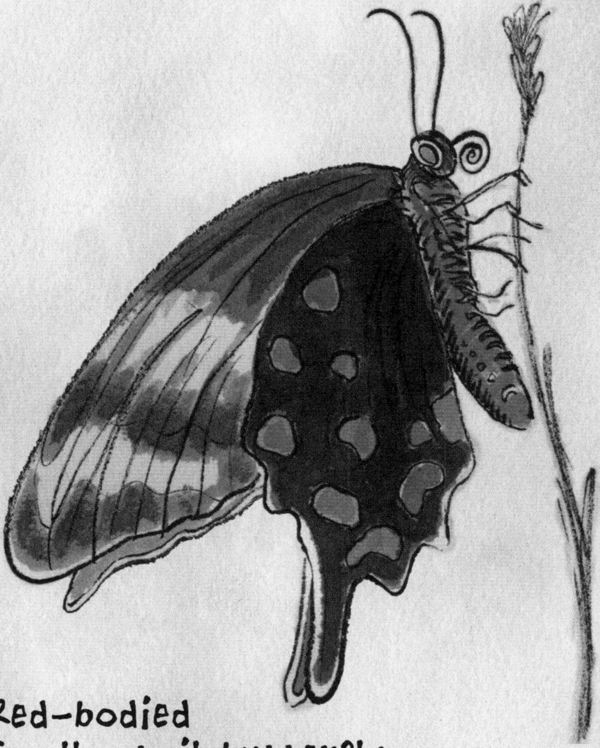

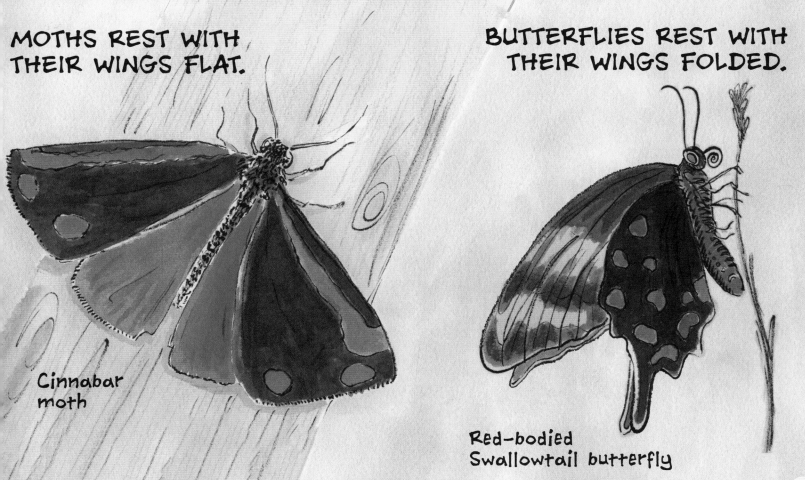

Red-bodied Swallowtail butterfly

MOTHS CAN BE BIG AND BEAUTIFUL.

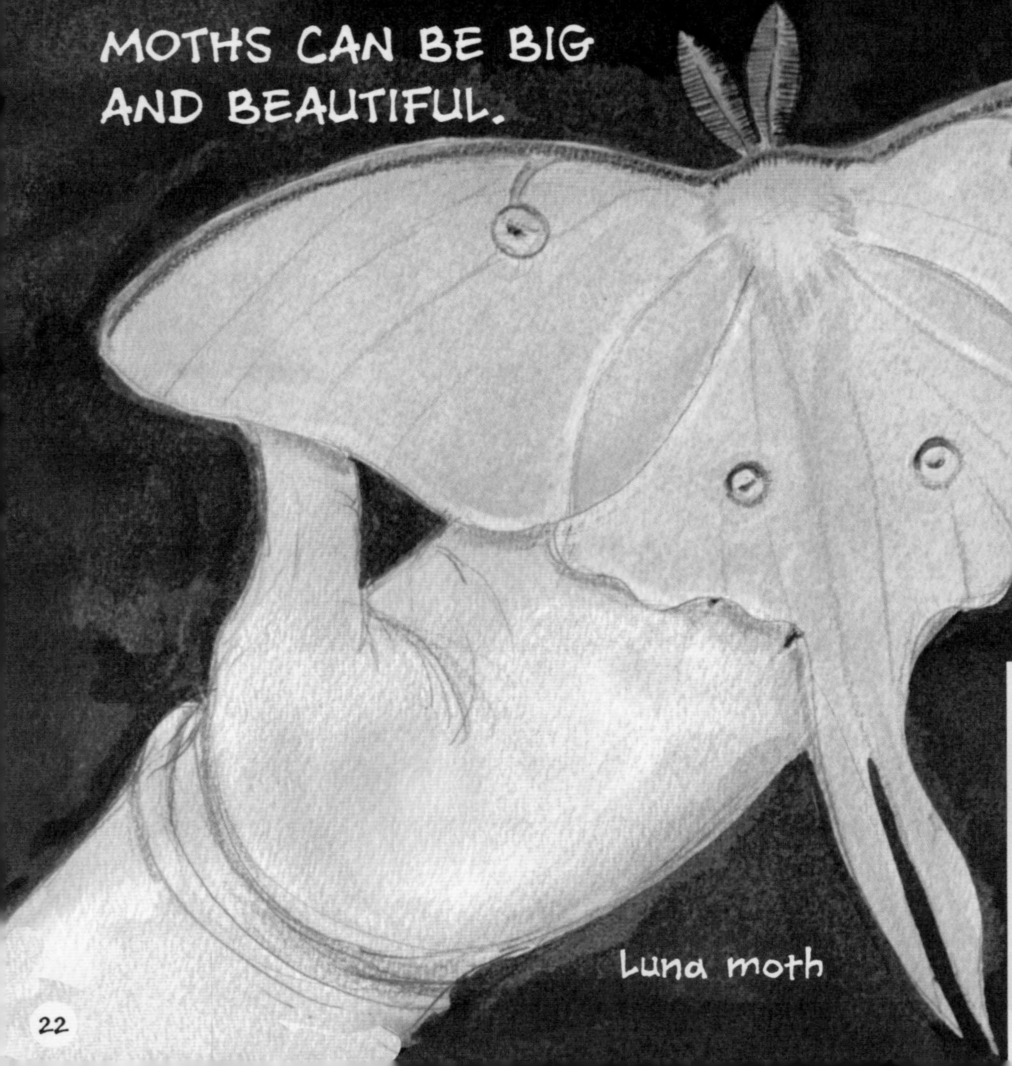

Luna moth

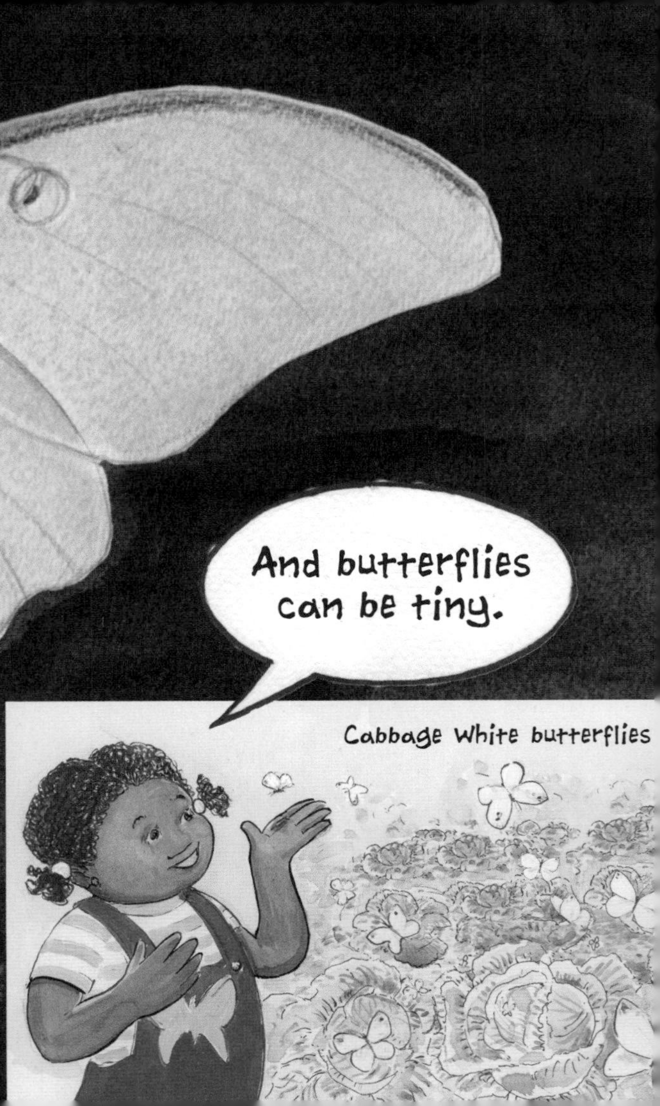
And butterflies can be tiny.

Cabbage White butterflies

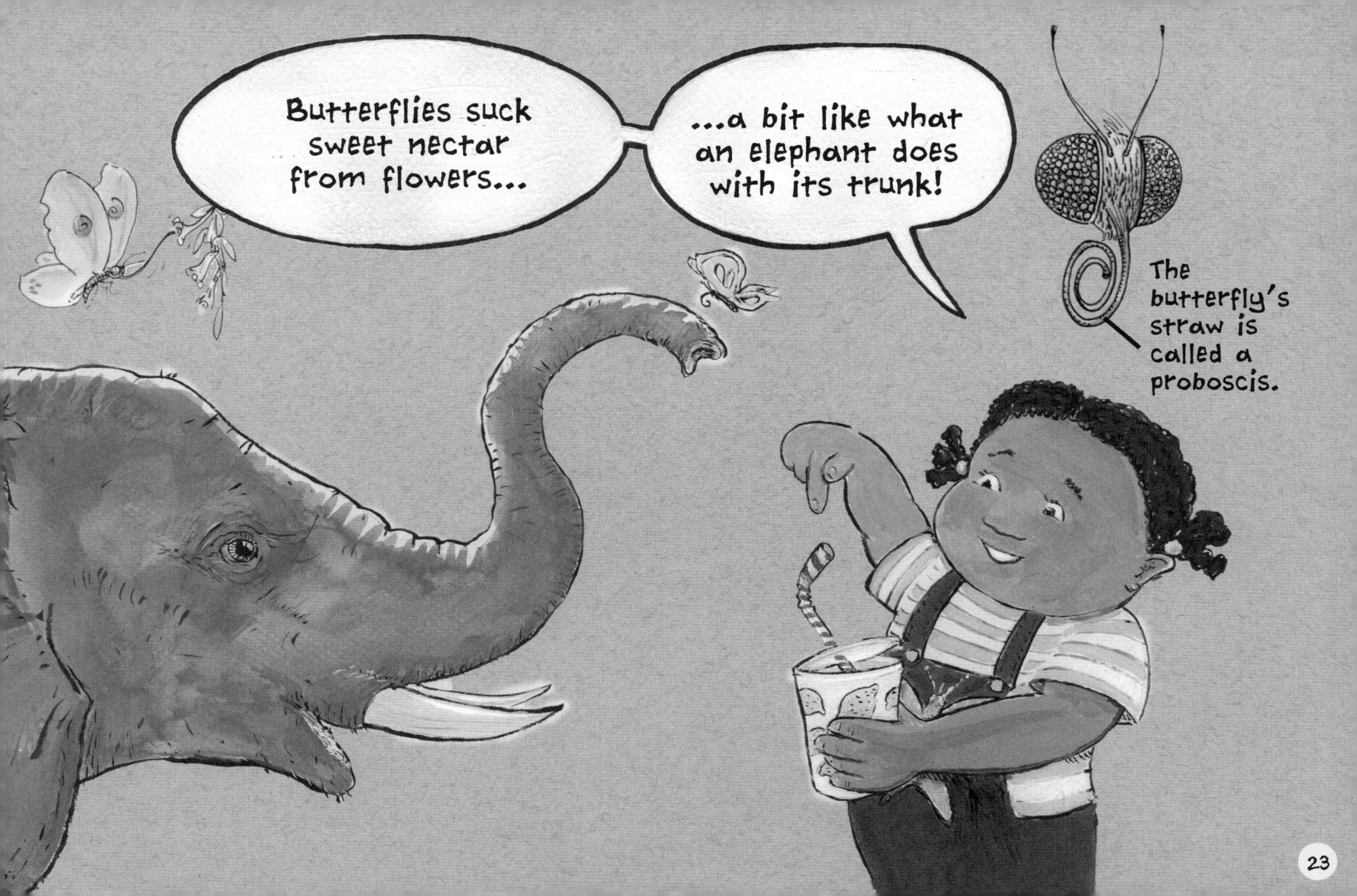
Butterflies suck sweet nectar from flowers...
...a bit like what an elephant does with its trunk!
The butterfly's straw is called a proboscis.

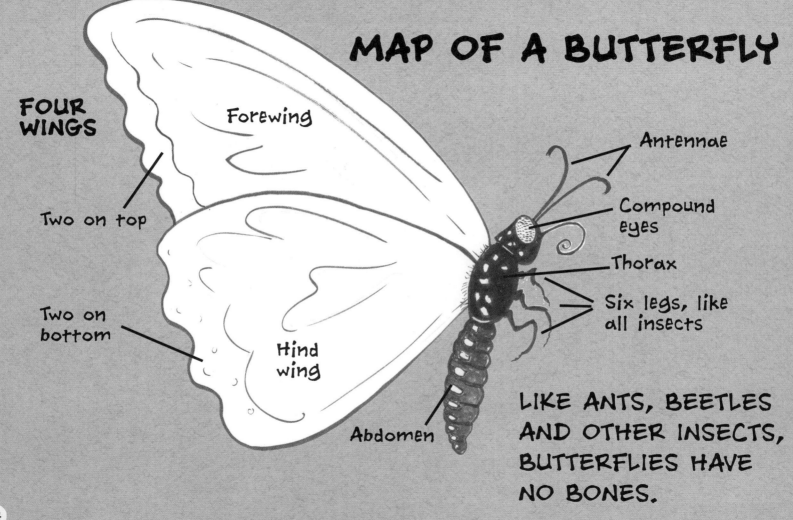

MAP OF A BUTTERFLY

FOUR WINGS

Forewing

Antennae

Compound eyes

Two on top

Thorax

Six legs, like all insects

Two on bottom

Hind wing

Abdomen

LIKE ANTS, BEETLES AND OTHER INSECTS, BUTTERFLIES HAVE NO BONES.

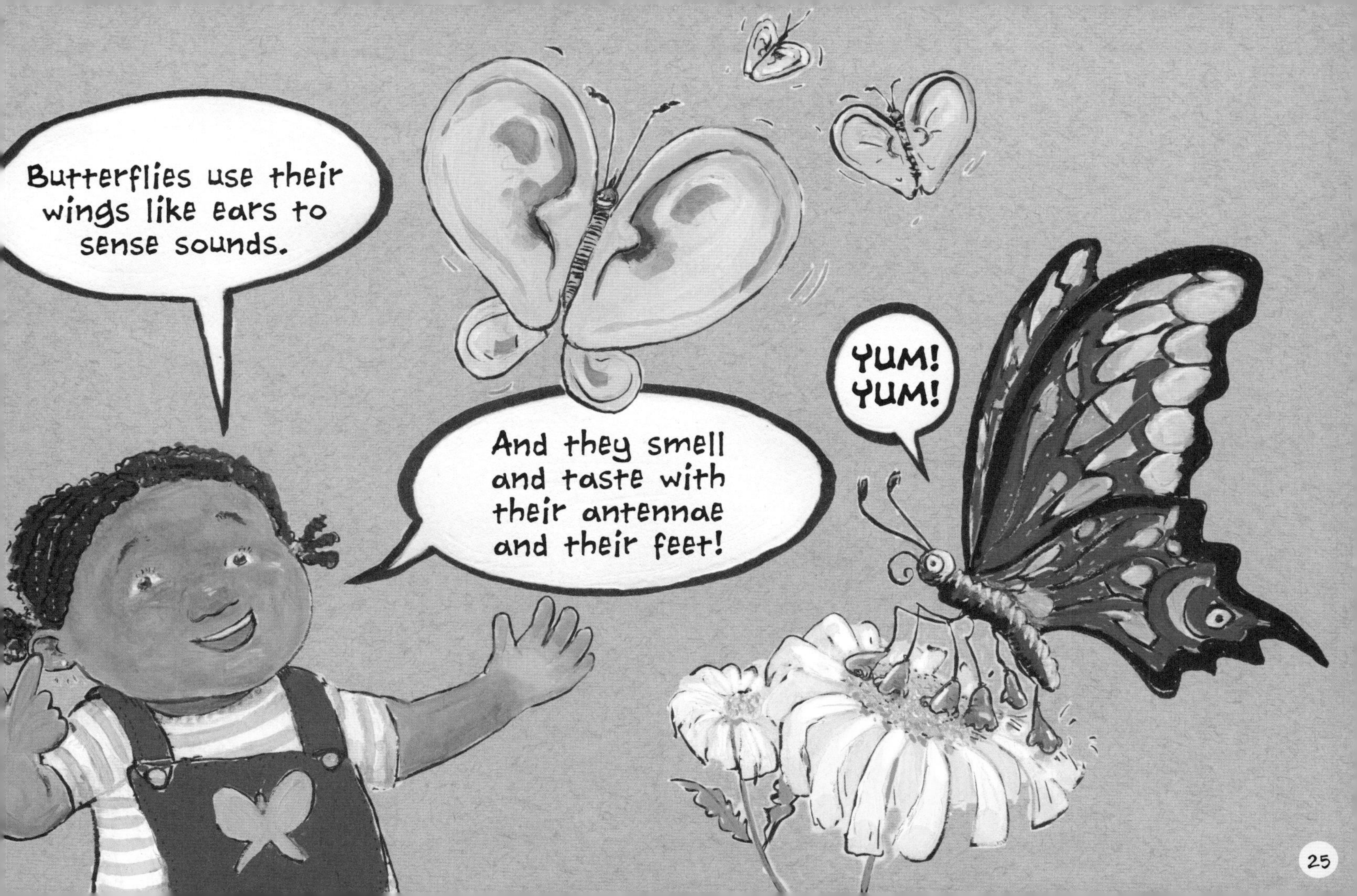
Butterflies use their wings like ears to sense sounds.
And they smell and taste with their antennae and their feet!
YUM! YUM!

BUTTERFLY WINGS ARE CLEAR.

Their color comes
from tiny scales
covering
the wings like
roof tiles.

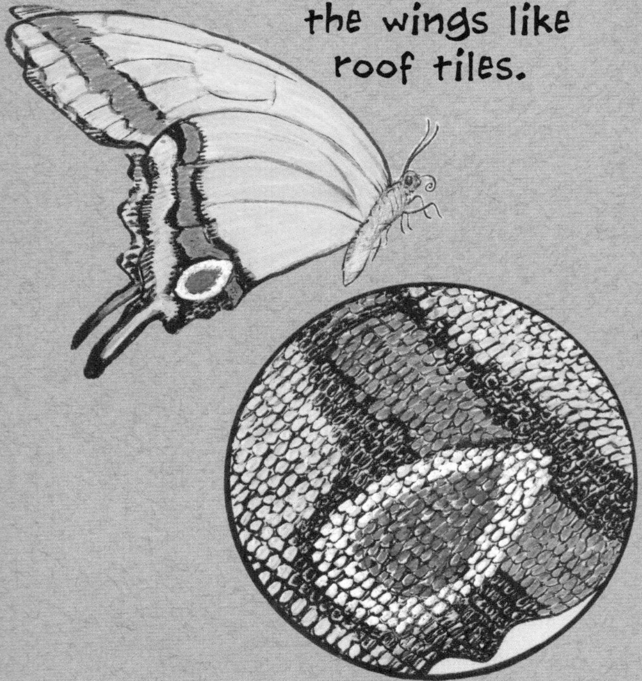

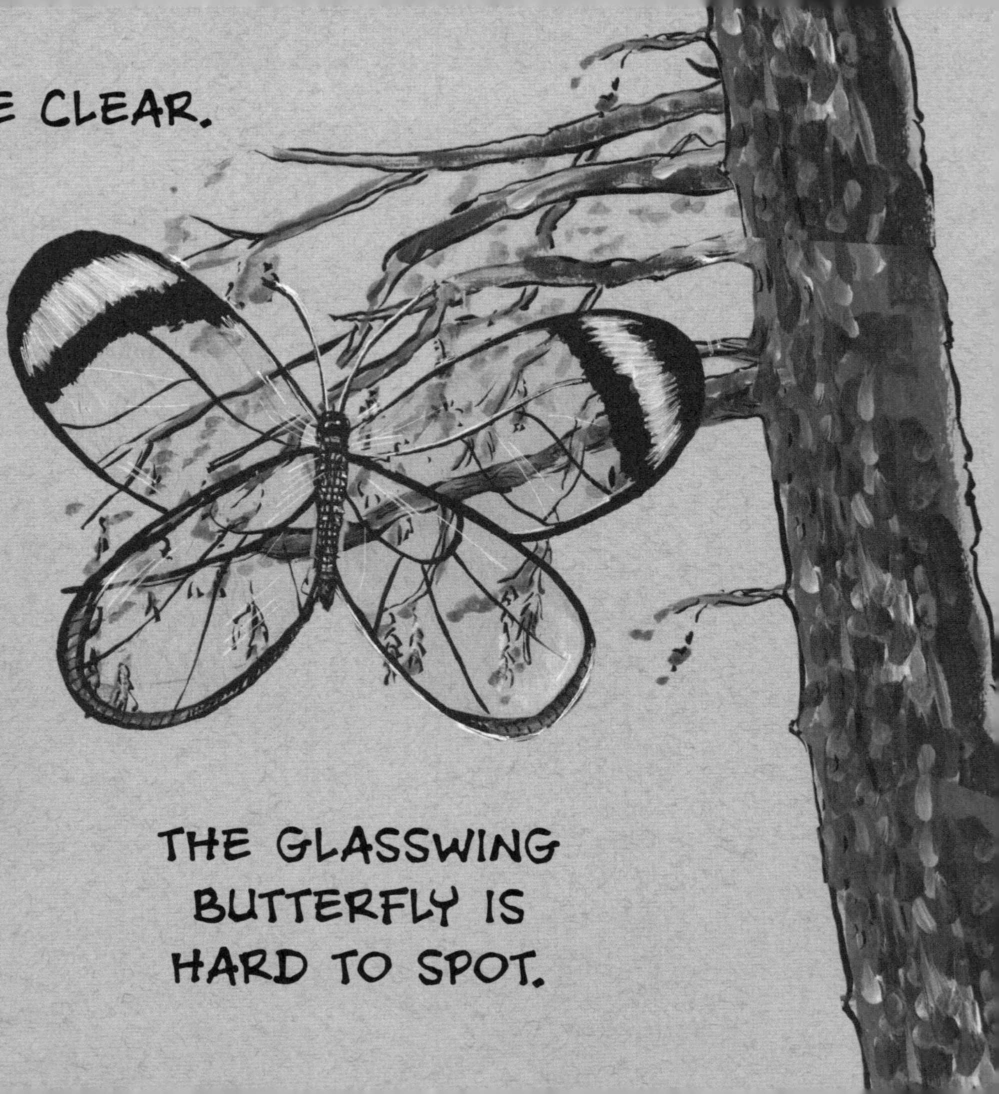

THE GLASSWING
BUTTERFLY IS
HARD TO SPOT.

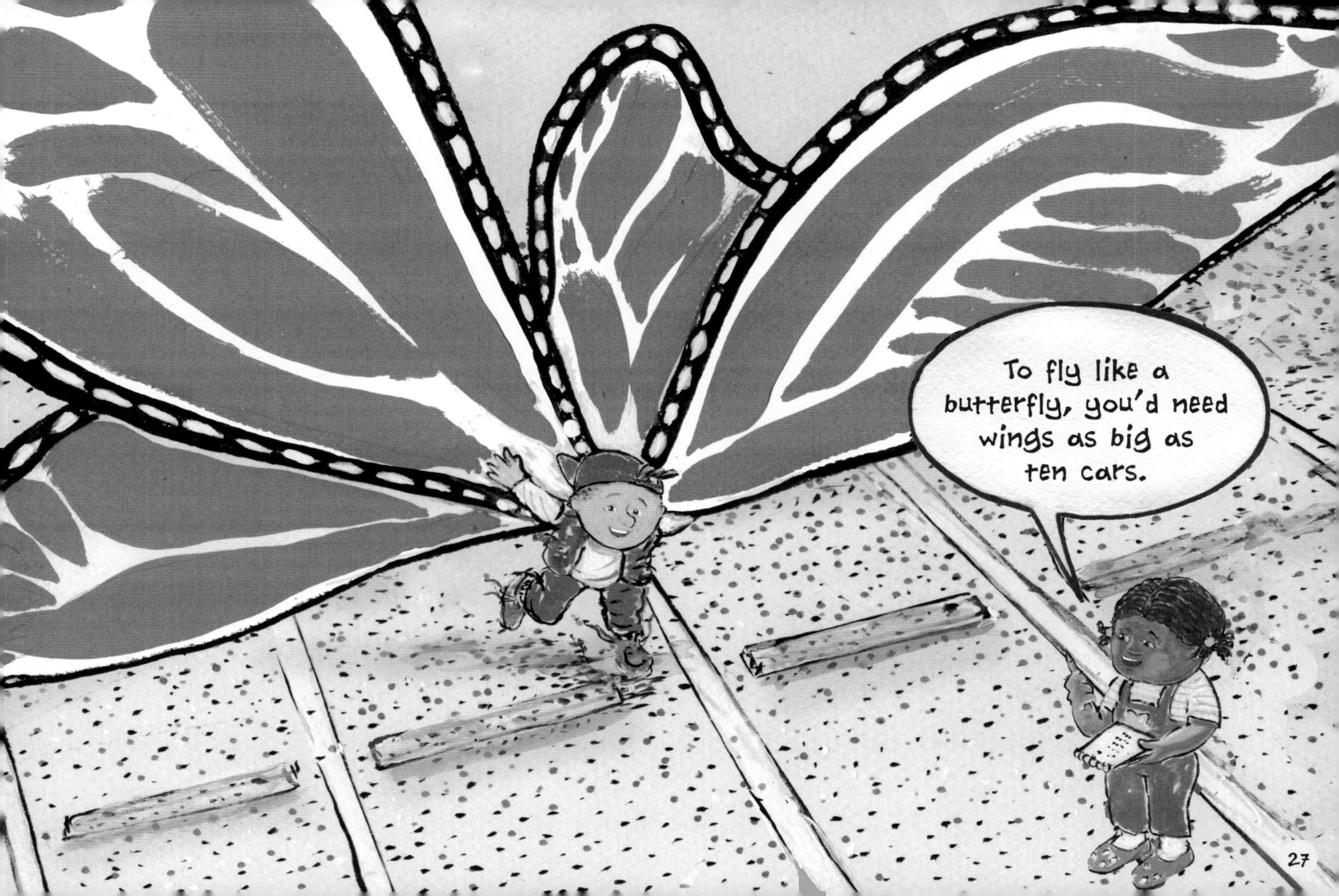
To fly like a butterfly, you'd need wings as big as ten cars.

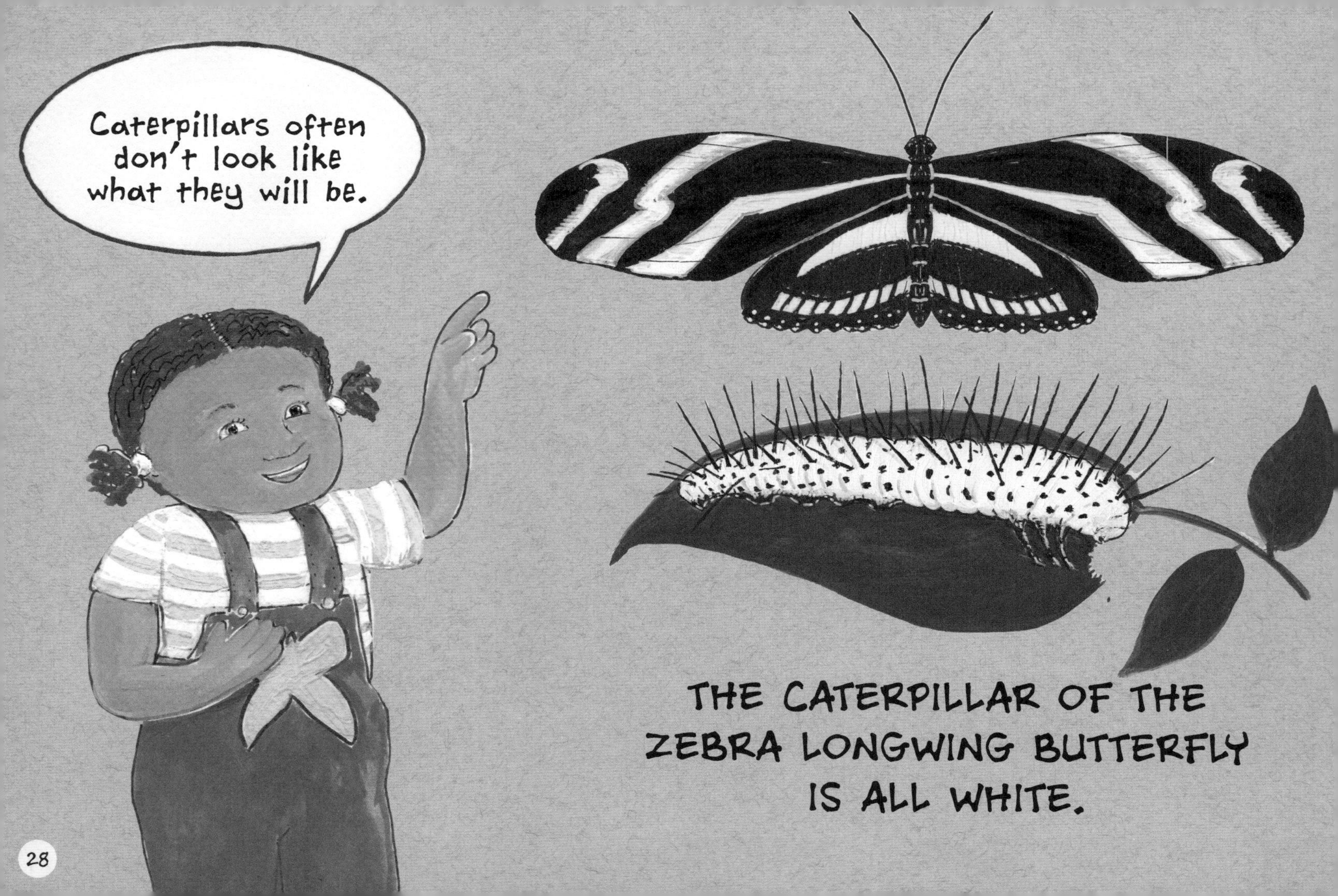
Caterpillars often don't look like what they will be.

THE CATERPILLAR OF THE ZEBRA LONGWING BUTTERFLY IS ALL WHITE.

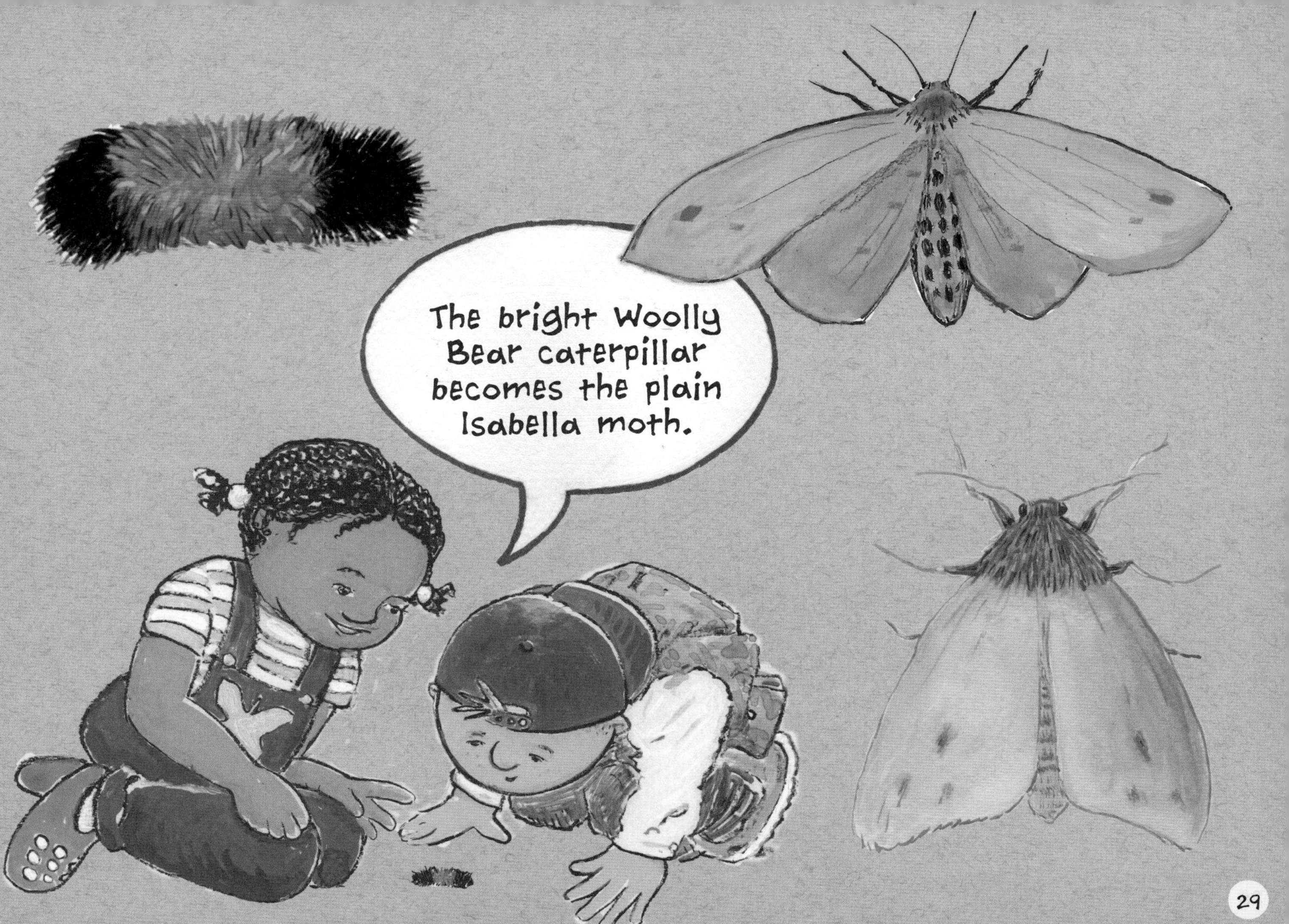
The bright Woolly Bear caterpillar becomes the plain Isabella moth.

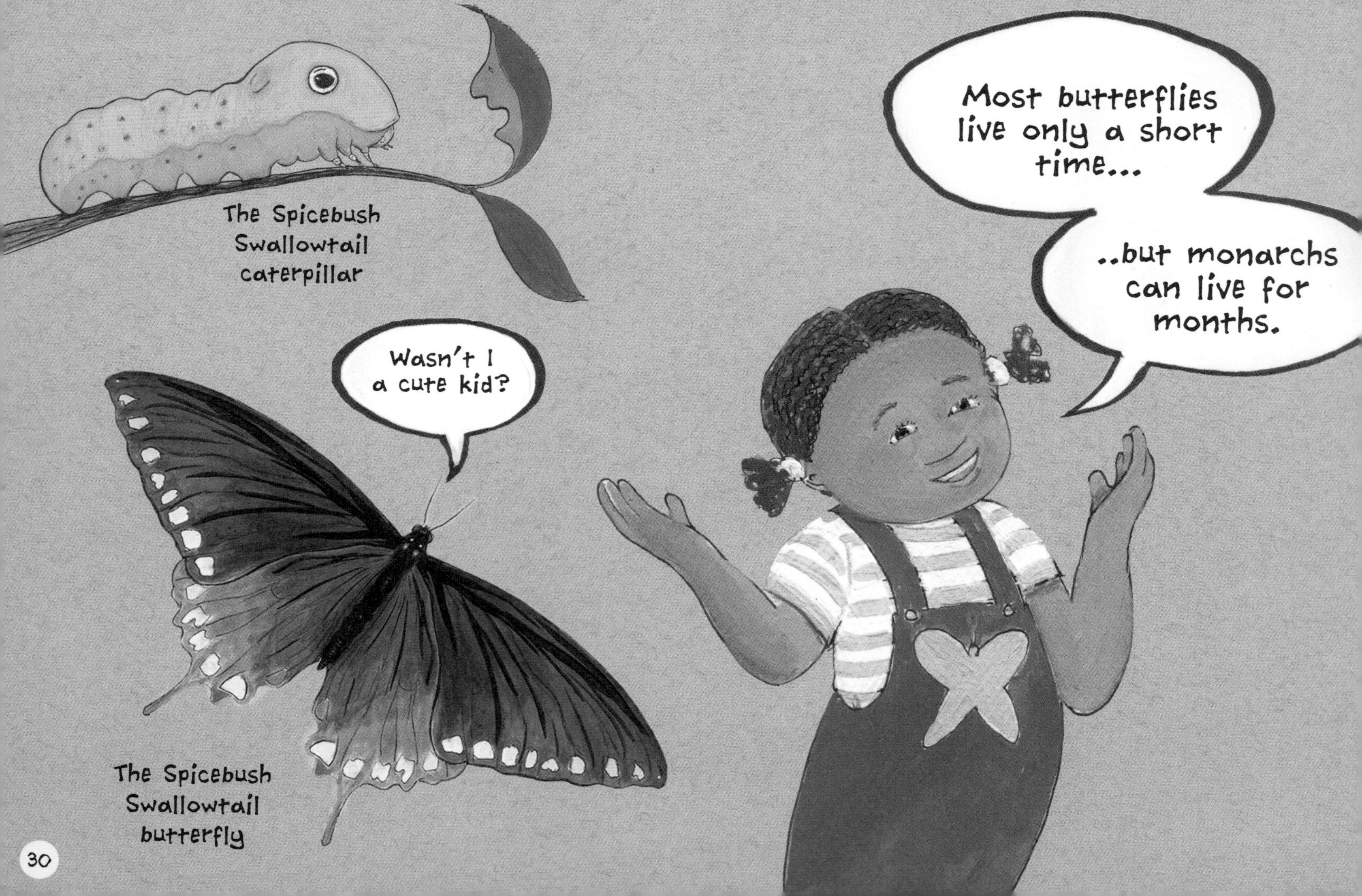

The Spicebush Swallowtail caterpillar
Wasn't I a cute kid?
The Spicebush Swallowtail butterfly
Most butterflies live only a short time...
..but monarchs can live for months.

SOME MONARCHS MIGRATE FOR THOUSANDS OF MILES.

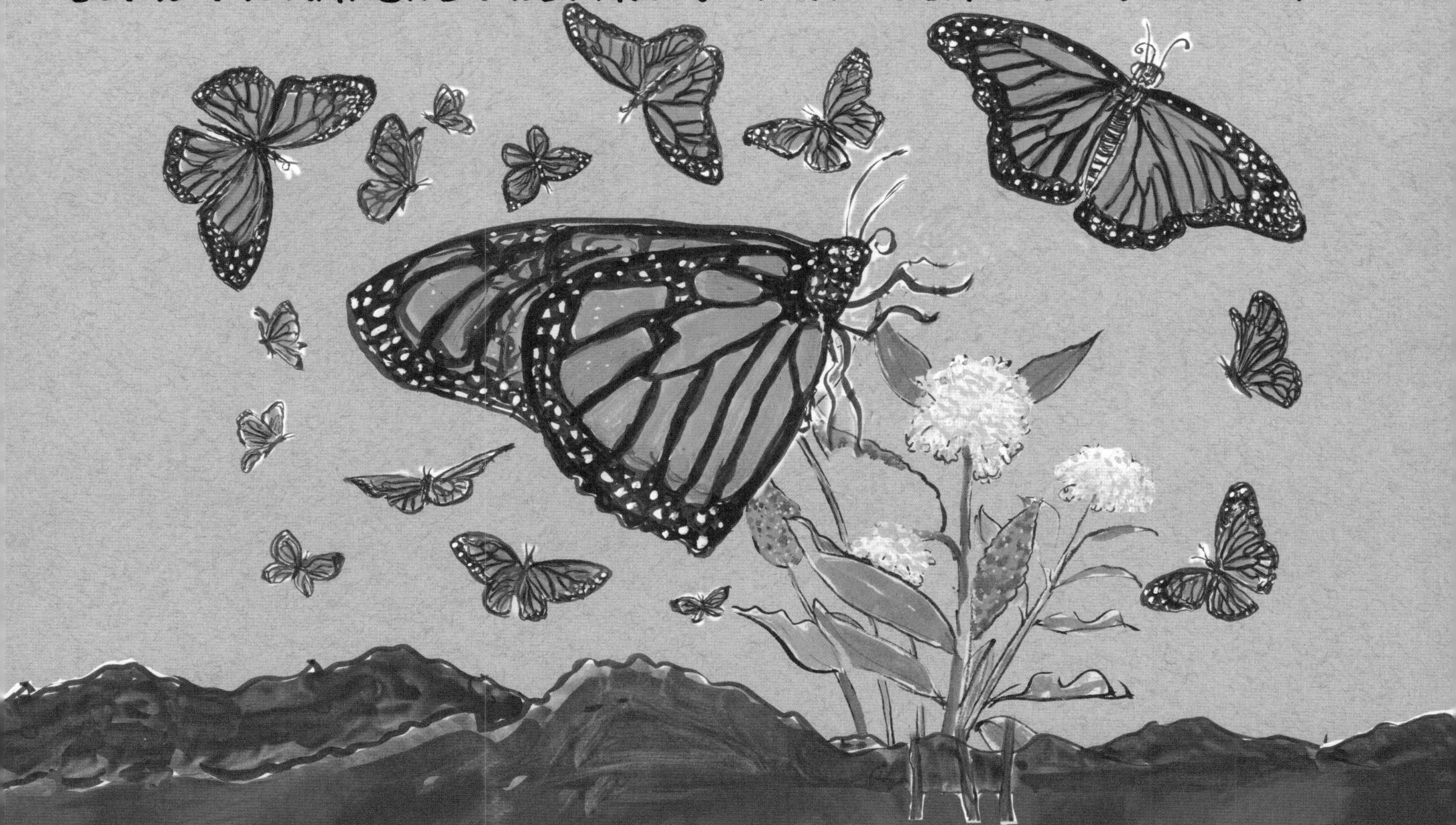

FROM THE USA OR CANADA, THEY FLY TO MEXICO FOR THE WINTER.

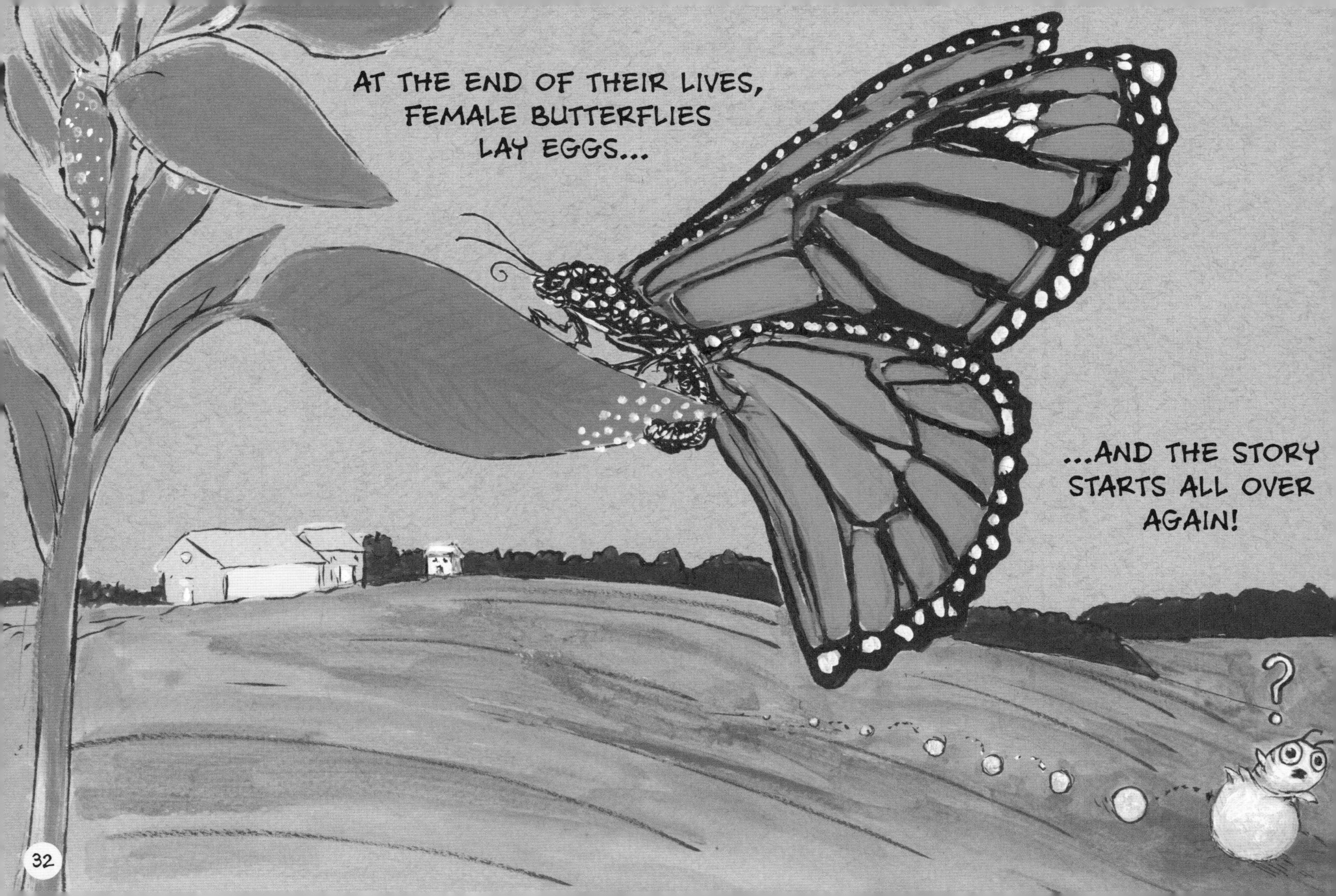
AT THE END OF THEIR LIVES, FEMALE BUTTERFLIES LAY EGGS...
...AND THE STORY STARTS ALL OVER AGAIN!
?

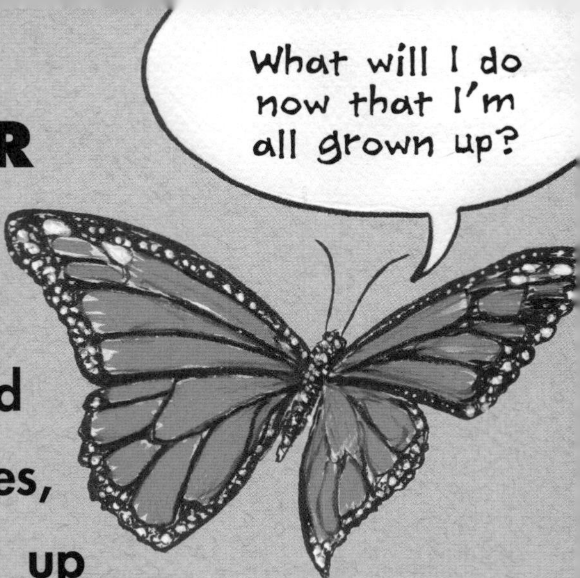
What will I do now that I'm all grown up?

ABOUT THE AUTHOR

When **KEVIN McCLOSKEY** was seven years old, he loved to ride his bike, paint pictures, and tell stories. He grew up and became a college professor, teaching art at Kutztown University for thirty years. Now Kevin is retired. He loves to ride his bike, paint pictures, and tell stories.

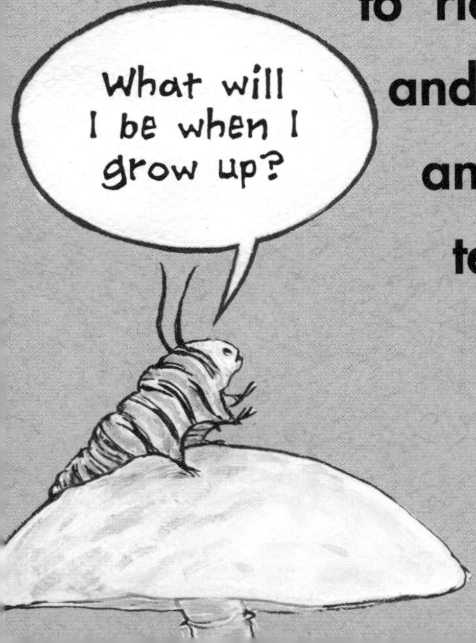
What will I be when I grow up?

HOW TO READ COMICS WITH KIDS

Kids love comics! They are naturally drawn to the details in the pictures, which make them want to read the words. Comics beg for repeated readings and let both emerging and reluctant readers enjoy complex stories with a rich vocabulary. But since comics have their own grammar, here are a few tips for reading them with kids:

GUIDE YOUNG READERS: Use your finger to show your place in the text, but keep it at the bottom of the character speaking so it doesn't hide the very important facial expressions.

HAM IT UP! Think of the comic book story as a play, and don't hesitate to read with expression and intonation. Assign parts or get kids to supply the sound effects, a great way to reinforce phonics skills.

LET THEM GUESS. Comics provide lots of context for the words, so emerging readers can make informed guesses. Like jigsaw puzzles, comics ask readers to make connections, so check children's understanding by asking, "What's this character thinking?" (But don't be surprised if a kid finds some of the comics' subtle details faster than you.)

TALK ABOUT THE PICTURES. Point out how the artist paces the story with pauses (silent panels) or speeded-up action (a burst of short panels). Discuss how the size and shape of the panels convey meaning.

ABOVE ALL, ENJOY! There is of course never one right way to read, so go for the shared pleasure. Once children make the story happen in their imagination, they have discovered the thrill of reading, and you won't be able to stop them. At that point, just go get them more books—and more comics!

www.TOON-BOOKS.com

SEE OUR FREE ONLINE CARTOON MAKERS, LESSON PLANS, AND MUCH MORE